Shock Therapy!

Building a Power Line
with a **BLONDE** Groundman

Kathleen Graham-Gandy

with

Charles E. Gandy

Books to Touch the Heart

Shock Inner Prizes Publishers
Mount Pleasant, Tennessee

Shock Therapy

By Kathleen Graham-Gandy
with Charles E. Gandy

Published by
Shock Inner Prizes, Inc.
Book Publishing Division
USA

Disclaimer: This book is in no way intended to make light of, or to degrade, linemen, groundmen or blondes.

ISBN: 0980081122
ISBN: 978-0980081121

Cover Design by: Charles E. Gandy,
Shock Inner Prizes, Inc.

TABLE OF CONTENTS

PREFACE

When Charley and I began discussing retirement, he laid a bombshell on me. He said, "It has always been a dream of mine to build my own power line." Well, being the supportive, loving wife that I am, I said, "Sure, Honey. We can do that." Little did I know what I was getting myself into.

The first day we went to his family's home place to "walk over" the property, I nearly fell three times. The walking over the property was a "spur of the moment" decision, and I was not prepared, as I was wearing old slick-soled tennis shoes (no hiking boots on this trip!). Right then, I wondered what the next several months would entail.

Charley has nearly 40 years of experience in the electric utility industry with an Electrical Engineering Degree. He has worked with power companies throughout his career. He has never been a lineman, but he has worked closely with all aspects of the job. He is a very thorough person and will study a project carefully before he starts…a real test of patience for a blonde "Git-R-Done" person.

Hermon Paul "Papaw" Gandy, Charley's father, helped us with building our power line and our cabin. Papaw worked construction jobs for many years with TVA. He, too, was a perfectionist. He was thrilled that Charley wanted to build on the home place, and he could not wait for us to get started. He helped us almost every day…well, every day that we could work on the project. But we will get into that more as the book develops…and he was always there, and waiting, when we arrived.

Oh, and my background? Well, I worked in the finance industry (i.e., banks and credit union) for almost 30 years. I am also a two-time cancer survivor. I had a melanoma in 1984, and I was diagnosed with breast cancer in 1996. For this latter, I had 33 radiation treatments and six chemotherapy treatments after a lumpectomy. Was I prepared to help my man fulfill his life-long dream? Sure. I was in it for the long haul...and it *was* a long haul.

We worked hard! We played hard! We laughed! We cried! We had lots of energy! We were exhausted...and hungry! And that was just the first day!

I kept a daily journal of our adventures...and adventures they were! I'm not sure why I kept this journal as I had never kept one before or since. With the passing of time, many of our adventures would have faded from memory without these journals to remind us of our daily activities. Read on to learn more about building a power line with a blonde groundman. And, men, I know that you will have sympathy for Charley as he had to work with me on a daily basis. After all, I am blonde...through and through...as the stories will reveal!!

Throughout this journey I was reminded often of Paul's words in Philippians 4:13 – "I can do all things through Christ which strengtheneth me" (KJV). And He did give us strength daily to accomplish the things that we needed to do for each task.

And to all of you blondes that may be reading this book – apart from the reality of these true-to-life experiences – we are not insulting your intelligence either. We all have to be willing to laugh at our own miscues and not be offended – whether Blonde, Brunette, or Redhead!

But from Blonde Bragging Rights, this *one* has done something – as you will read – that most Brunettes and Redheads have not done. So, take it from this blonde: We Blondes can do anything we set our minds to – if we work at it hard enough!

Now as to doing anything…well, this experience of building a power line is one that would be strictly forbidden without proper expertise to accomplish the same – safely. So as they say on all the daredevil and reality shows on TV…

DO NOT ATTEMPT THIS AT HOME!

ACKNOWLEDGMENTS

Thank you to my sister, Pat LaFern, whose untiring work helped us to get our cabin built. She brought food to the work site many times which allowed me a brief respite from having to decide what food to take to feed the workers. Her willingness to come to the woods to help us meant so much to us…especially as she and Jerry had to travel a good distance to get to the site. And, her devotion to our project went far beyond a sister's obligation.

Along with that, she also helped us to move into the cabin, and six months later helped us move again, as our lives went yet another direction.

Thanks, too, to Jan Best for editing this book for us. And, also, for the many phone calls, and always listening when I talked about the book constantly. As always, you are "The Best" at whatever you do. We appreciate your willingness to review our books for us.

And, a HUGE thanks to Charley, my husband, my soul mate, my best friend, for once again helping me to fulfill my life-long dream yet again, by writing this book. This book has a special meaning to me as it is living proof that we can do whatever we set our minds to do…with the Lord's help. Charley, you truly are "the wind beneath my wings."

IN MEMORY

This book is dedicated to the memory of the following people:

Hermon Paul (Papaw) Gandy, Charley's Dad. Our power line would not have become a reality without his wisdom to help us through some very sticky situations. His support kept us encouraged and on track, and his humor allowed us to remember that it was all in a day's work, and to keep things in perspective. His zeal of building and raising the cabin walls fulfilled a life-long dream, as if it was his very own.

Hester Mae Butler Gandy, Charley's mom, who would have loved to have been a part of this adventure, but she had already gone to be with the Lord before we moved back home to Tennessee.

Jerry LaFern, our brother-in-law, who helped us build the cabin, contributed to the electrical work, and advised us on the mechanical issues of our tractor. His wisdom and expertise were priceless.

Bud Staggs, Charley's cousin, who helped us with building the cabin and many other projects along the way, even at a moment's notice.

Donnie Will and Edna Earl Mosley Graham, my parents, who taught me that perseverance is the key to finishing any project.

IN HONOR

This book is also dedicated to linemen everywhere who risk their lives on a daily basis, so that we may enjoy our conveniences. This book is not intended to make light of their hard work, but to recognize their dedication to the jobs they love. Thank you, Linemen, wherever you are, for all that you do. May God richly bless each one of you and your families. (The families of these men [and women] are often left alone at the darkest of times, so that the linemen can go out into the storms to bring us light.)

CHAPTER I
The Vision

Picture it: Brush Creek, Hohenwald, Tennessee. The date is Saturday, February 6, 1999. Charley and I, looking forward to retirement in a few months, decided to drive down to the family property in Lewis County, Tennessee, to determine where we wanted to build our cabin.

Charley, standing on the side of the hill at the spot he selected, could envision the full picture: A cabin with two full sides surrounded with a railed deck; an off-shoot deck leading down to the 10-acre lake's edge with small cabins dotting the perimeter of the lake for use by ministers and youth groups; a small island in the center of the lake for overnight camping; a rock-enclosed spring with an abundant flow of heavenly-pure water streaming out of the hillside; a 2800-foot power line fed at 2400 volts – stepped up at a meter pole near Dad's house in Lewis County and stepped back down at the cabin pole, and..."Yes, I'll be right there," as Kathy summoned Charley from his engrossed daydream of "The Vision". The day was cloudy with temperature of about 60 degrees, a nice, warm day in middle Tennessee for February.

Not realizing that a drive to the property would entail an all-day hike over hundreds of acres of hilly forest land, I found myself in well-seasoned slick-soled tennis shoes...hardly the attire for our changed, and challenging, adventure of the day. My trusty hiking boots – left at home in Bowling Green, Kentucky – would have made this hike a "piece of cake."

Well, to say I was having some problems maneuvering the hillsides was definitely an understatement. Avoiding falls in the many tree-stump holes which were conveniently ground-leveled with the tons of leaves from the dense forest, made each step a "mine field" of rural adventure. After the third tumble, Charley asked me if I was okay. And, of course, my response was, "Oh sure, sure," but words were shallow as I envisioned the chal-

lenges that must lie ahead...and little did I know.

But having been raised a farm girl in rural Giles County, Tennessee, I finally began to admit that my farm days were long since passed, and city life of the past 30 years had softened my rustic finish. So, was I really up to the challenge of building a cabin...and power line? Only time would tell! But we have committed, and – as with our full life – what Charley and I commit to, WE DO...with the Good Lord's help!

The excitement of retirement, moving back home, and being closer to family, helped to spur us on. We could not wait to get started on this new chapter of our lives...and what a chapter it would become!

After having trekked through the woods all day, fighting gnats and other woodsy insects, we decided to grab a bite to eat at a "nearby restaurant." Yes, even though we were deep in the woods on the banks of Brush Creek, there was the Natchez Trace about two miles away, a major highway (US 64) within another five miles, and then west on US 64, a nice restaurant resided on the bank of Forty-eight Creek which was about an additional four miles...and thus the nearby restaurant, *The Country Store & Steakhouse*.

I remember telling Charley that I was dirty, sweaty and not dressed for going out, but his famous words that resounded many times over the next two years rang out: "Don't worry. We won't see anyone we know!"

Well, as soon as we entered the restaurant, we were greeted by Charley's niece, Jackie; her husband, Tommy; and their daughter, Lindsey (who was celebrating her twelfth birthday)...all in their neatly dressed attire. I tried not to think about how we must have looked after our all-day hike.

During the meal we talked with them a while and told them what we had been up to that day, pointing out the fact that we were retiring and moving back to the area. We spoke about our plans of building a cabin on the family home place. Charley discussed with Tommy about possibly helping him with the power line to our new cabin. (Tommy was a lineman for the neighboring Lawrenceburg Power System.) We shared our excitement about having our own little haven in the woods. Jackie called us "Hermon's Hermits," Charley's dad being named Hermon. The name stuck and we decided to call our place "Hermon's Hermits' Haven."

So to tie the hidden haven to the outside world we decided to name our mile-long "lane" to the cabin: Triple 'H' Lane, the title shortened so as to not create too much tie with the outside world under the pretense of being the '60s rock group, Herman's Hermits. Now we envisioned the beautiful sign at the road junction "Triple 'H' Lane" and "Gandy Road", just off the Natchez Trace in the northwest corner of Lawrence County.

The first professional sign for our road, Triple 'H'

 Lane, lasted all of one week. The second professional sign, a duplication of the first, lasted about two weeks. And then someone explained to us that "Triple H" was the name of a famous professional wrestler of the day. (We are never too old to learn!)

The third rustic sign, put up by Charley's brother, Paul, simply read, "Trple H Ln" on a rough piece of tin...and still shabbily resides on the same post today. I guess it wasn't fancy enough for someone to steal!

The area is definitely remote as it is located near a three-county junction near TWRA: Lewis, Lawrence, and Wayne Counties. There are woods on every side with no likelihood of anyone moving next door. Laurel Hill Wildlife Reserve is adjacent to the family property. It is truly a "haven in the woods." After working in the professional world for thirty-plus years, we were definitely ready to get away from it all.

The following day, Sunday, February 7, we returned to the property for a short while, before we ventured back toward Bowling Green from our weekend retreat, Stonebrook Lodge, just west of Waynesboro. Two wise conclusions came from our much-needed rest following yesterday's venture:

> (1) The road must be widened before any construction could begin on the cabin or power line. This historical road, the old Columbia-Ashland Highway, was a small, one-lane, log road that had several sharp turns to dodge with certain fixated roots that refused to yield to any tire or equipment that chose to straighten the journey along the "highway."
>
> (2) The cabin site must be cleared of trees before any building could be started. Remember, this setting is in the thick of the woods with no civilization in this area since the 1940s when Charley's grandparents had a small house on the upper place. An early bootlegger also lived in a house in the corner of the bottom.

The day was beautiful and sunny with the temperature in the mid-60s, and a strong wind blowing.

We continued our day's venture by looking around the area for rental property in which to live, while we built our cabin and power line. Since there were no rental properties in the south-end of Lewis County near Papaw's place, we decided to drive toward the nearest civilized community along US Highway 64 in Lawrence County, about eight miles from the cabin site. We silently prayed that the Good Lord would give us favor, and to our surprise, He did. *(Amusing that we pray, believing God will answer, and then we are blown away when He does. It is so hard for this flesh to grasp His greatness.)*

The first country store, where we stopped to inquire of rental property, was a family-owned establishment. The daughter, Stephanie, owned a 14' X 80' trailer that would be vacated at precisely the time that we needed it. After looking at the trailer, we accepted the offer and locked it in for the projected date. Neighbors to the trailer property, Ricky and Pam, were renting the trailer while they finished some renovation projects on their own home.

Later we found out that Ricky was a brick-and-block mason, and one of the best – and cheapest – in Lawrence County. *(Isn't that just like God? You pray a simple earnest prayer and before you get it out of your mouth, He's answered that prayer and the next one before it was even prayed. He truly does know what we have need of even before we pray...but He does like for us to ask just to acknowledge our Source of supply.)* It turned out that

Ricky and Pam were a little delayed on finishing the work on their home, but it worked out great because Charley and I had to do some repairs and painting to our Bowling Green home before we could fully prepare for its sale.

My last day of work at Service One Credit Union (formerly WKU Credit Union) was March 31, and Charley's last day at Bowling Green Municipal Utilities was April 30. Before moving to Lawrenceburg in May, Charley and I spent all of April and most of May doing repairs, maintenance, and general over-haul of the house in Bowling Green. We worked 16 – to – 18 hour days. We painted, put down new floor covering, repaired walls and windows, and washed windows. Our days were long and hard.

Charley planted flowers and sowed grass seed. The temperatures during this time were in the mid-to-upper 80s. The house and yard had never looked better. We were very pleased with how everything looked. We had hoped to sell the house before moving, but it did not happen.

The decision was made. It was time to move to Tennessee and get started on clearing the land for our cabin. But, prior to the non-stop working project, Charley and I took a few days off (May 17 – 19) to go to Gulf Shores, Alabama with my sister, Pat, and her husband, Jerry. We also attended the high school graduation of a nephew, Scottie, on May 20, returning to Bowling Green after the ceremony.

On May 25, we rented a U-Haul truck and headed for our new temporary residence at the trailer. *(Another prayer answered before it was prayed: the delay of Ricky and Pam's moving allowed us to delay paying about four months of rent prior to our arrival.)* The beginning statement sounded so simple – load up and move. But my journals did not depict that simplicity. On Wednesday, May 25, 1999, we rented a U-Haul truck to move to 48 Smith Road, Lawrenceburg, Tennessee. We planned to be packed and "on the road" by noon on the 26th, but it did not happen.

Charley and I disassembled the remaining furniture, and loaded everything on the truck by ourselves. We rented the truck at noon on the 25th which meant we needed to have it returned to Lawrenceburg, Tennessee by noon on the 27th. We had two days to load the truck in Bowling Green and then unload the truck at our trailer in Lawrence County. Plenty of time to do all that was needed…or so we thought.

We loaded boxes all afternoon on the 25th; however, we had several neighbors who came by to bid us farewell and offer their help. Charley politely told them we could do it with no problem. *(Isn't it just like a man to turn down the help that the Good Lord sends us? Of course, Charley being 80% deaf knows that hearing and work do not go hand in hand since 95% of his hearing is lip read-ing. So if he's listening, he's not working, and if he's working, he's not listening...thus the refusal of help, knowing the deadline we were to meet.)*

After about half the boxes were loaded, Charley came up with the idea to take down the banister on the top of the stairs, lay braces and plywood over the stairs, and slide the boxes down the ramp. It was amazing how much faster and easier the project became. I tied a rope around a box, held on to the rope while the box slid down the ramp, then Charley would untie the rope and load the box on the truck. If it was a heavy box or a piece of furniture, we would reverse roles, so that I was not racing with the load as it headed for the ground floor. And then we both would load it on the truck. We lowered each box or piece of furniture slowly…very slowly.

We worked all day on the 26th and were able to leave around 5 PM, the noon deadline having long since passed with each neighbors' visit. But their offers and caring gave us the strength to endure the day. Some even brought food and drink for us, as we were too busy to stop to get something for ourselves.

The most difficult pieces were the piano and the freezer. The piano almost rolled off the ramp to the truck, but Charley caught it just before reaching the "point of no return" and crushing me underneath. At 115 pounds I was no match for a 300-pound piano toppling off the ramp at a high rate of speed.

Something that had really helped us was that before we started packing up, we had purchased two four-wheel

dollies and a two-wheel dolly. These prevented us from
having to do a lot of lifting. One additional thing that
helped to simplify our day's work of moving a four bedroom house of furnishings to a three bedroom trailer is
the fact that prior to today's move, we had rented two
sizeable storage units and placed all non-pertinent furniture and surplus in those facilities…a two month's process.

   As we began our journey southward, we refused to
stop before getting through the heavy traffic of Nashville
and even I-65 South, knowing our meal would not digest
with that pressure still ahead of us. I was just ahead of
Charley, so I pulled over on the interstate just south of
Franklin (Tennessee) to wait until he caught up to me.
As I was sitting there watching for Charley, a Tennessee
Highway Patrolman turned on his blue lights and pulled
in behind me. Of course, my heart was beating so loudly
that I was afraid that the trooper could hear it over the
sounds of the interstate traffic. I could barely breathe, as
I waited for him to tell me what I had done wrong. But he
was only checking to see if everything was alright. He
was very nice and polite. Whew! I was able to breathe
again. When I saw Charley approaching me, I gave my
signal so that I could merge in with the traffic. We waited until we reached Columbia – about 7:00 p.m. – and
stopped at Taco Bell for supper. I couldn't wait to tell
him that a THP had stopped to check on me. We finally
arrived at the trailer at 8:30. We were too tired to do

anything more, so we went to bed (in one of our previously moved beds).

On Thursday, May 27, Charley and I got up around 6:00 a.m. and began to unload the truck as it had to be returned to Lawrenceburg by noon. The ramp on the truck was even with the top step of the trailer, so everything went very smoothly, even the piano. We left for Lawrenceburg at 11:15 and had the truck turned in by 11:45, with fifteen minutes to spare. Although the trailer had three bedrooms, we used the two smaller ones for storage – each room packed to the brim.

Having been a couple months focused on our roadway and house site preparation, on Saturday, August 14, 1999 – after our sons left following their birthday lunch – we went to the cabin site, which was our first visit since the dozer work had been completed (see Chapter Two).

Charley worked on the two water springs flowing out of the hillside just below the cabin site, to determine which would be the best to use for drinking water for the cabin. There was one formation that was solid rock with dimensions of 13 inches wide by 33 inches long by 15 inches deep, with a 5 inch by 11 inch rock run-off. The temperature was perfect today with low 80s and a cool breeze.

On Sunday, August 15, we went to church at Center Grove Church of God, having found this community church only about five miles from our trailer. We visited several churches before we found this one that would become our home church for several years.

Pat and Jerry came over about 1:30 and we all went down to the property. We showed them the house place and where the two springs were located. They liked the layout that we had planned, along with the privacy and all the adventures the woods had to offer.

Pat and Jerry were our first "company" to the cabin site. The temperature was in the mid-80s and just a great day. We went back to church for evening services. When we returned home Charley worked on the layout of the property on paper so we could do a "survey" on Monday.

On Monday, August 16, Charley and I surveyed a plot of land approximately 20 acres or so in size, so his dad could deed it to us, paving the way for us to build our cabin. We walked up hills, down hills, over the branch and across the creek. It was a very hot day with temperatures in the upper 90s. It took us about five hours to walk the property and flag the lines.

When we returned home we put six quarts of applesauce in the freezer from apples that Papaw gave us from his tree. *(Today our youngest son, Derek, is 20 years old. Sure makes a woman feel old...but no time for feeling old – there's work to be done!)*

Early on Tuesday morning we had to re-do one line of the survey because we came up short on one side. Papaw was having a problem with his tractor, so Charley helped him while I stayed at Papaw's house to fix lunch for all of us.

We spent the afternoon working on the paper layout of the survey. Papaw disked the ground at the upper place during the morning and the bottom in the afternoon. It took about two hours to do the disking...but longer to fix the tractor. We seemed to work more on the tractor than the project at hand! Temperature today was in the upper 90s and very hot...that old tractor may be smarter than we are...just quit for the day!

On Thursday, August 26, Charley and Papaw went to the cabin site to look at the springs for our cabin. Papaw suggested that he should "tie" the two springs together since they were only 15 feet apart and that should supply plenty of water to the cabin. I did a "catch up day" by doing Papaw's laundry and cleaning his house. I also cooked lunch for all of us. We actually had a slow day and returned home early. After supper we walked a couple of miles. The day was perfect and in the 80s.

On Monday, August 30, our realtor called. She was at the house (in Bowling Green) with prospective buyers and had questions. *(Unfortunately, the house did not sell at that time.)*

On Friday, September 10, we went to Hohenwald to pick up the survey for the twenty acres. We then rode toward Linden to see if we could locate the Mennonites who built storage buildings. We needed somewhere to store our tools so that we did not have to transport them back and forth every day, and we thought that perhaps we would get one built. On Saturday we went to Papaw's to show him the survey and give him a copy.

On Thursday, September 23, 1999, we went to Bowling Green to get my 401K. We met with our realtor to see if she had any updates on the sale of our house, and then came home. We still did not have any prospects for our house. The mortgage payment on the Bowling Green house, rent on the trailer, rent on storage units, and funding of the cabin (and all its construction costs), were wreaking havoc with our finances...and thus the need of the 401K.

On Saturday, February 12, 2000 we returned to Bowling Green and got the rest of our things from the storage units and the house. The temperature was in the 30s and it was cold with snow flurries! We unloaded the truck on Sunday afternoon.

Charley became sick with the flu around the 13th. We worked a couple of days that week, but he was not able to work anymore until Monday, February 21. He was very sick with a high temperature, coughing, and chills. He stayed in bed or in the recliner most of the time. I begged him to wait until he was completely over the flu before getting back to work in the fields, but he would not listen. He lost fifteen pounds while he was sick. He looked frail and felt sluggish, but he believed that we could not stop...the work had to be finished. (*Isn't that just like a man to think that even though he is sick he has to keep going and not take the time to recuperate?*)

Charley was only able to work a few hours the first day after being so sick. It took him about a week to get his strength to the point where he could work longer hours. And even then at night he was too exhausted to do more than take a bath and go to bed. I had to force him to eat to get his strength back.

On February 22, 2000, we finally obtained a contract on our house in Bowling Green! We were very excited! It was scheduled to close by March 6. We prayed hard that there would be no problems, and everything would go as scheduled.

The house did close on Tuesday, March 7. A few problems arose prior to the closing, but those problems were ironed out and the closing went smoothly. It was so good to have that behind us and to have extra finances available so that we could survive and continue with the power line and cabin. Although part of our financial burden was relieved, the delay had created some credit accumulation that needed resolving.

Charley's thought: So the simple solution now was to borrow a small amount against the cabin, so funds would be available for completing the project...Right? Wrong! Kathy, with her 12-15 years in mortgage lending management, could not fault the banker. If you want help with a home, you borrow before you start the project...or after you finish...not in the middle! (Too bad our crystal ball was broken, and we could not see the year's delay of the house sale. Otherwise, we would have borrowed the money at the beginning of the process. Had the house sold prior to leaving Bowling Green, we would have had plenty of funds to complete our building project, but again, we had no way to see the future.)

So the <u>other</u> simple solution: What about a personal loan? "No problem," said the banker. "We can do that with a signature loan – little to no collateral – and several thousand dollars above what you were asking as a mortgage loan." Made sense to me, who cared about the logic ...or lack thereof! Just show me the money!

On Monday, April 3, Charley bought a tractor. He had only driven Papaw's 1948 Farmall, which was instrumental in teaching Charley to drive a vehicle, but he knew that Papaw's tractor with straight steering and no three-point attachment could ever measure up in saved labor of the later models with power steering and hydraulic three-point hitch.

Charley had seen an ad in the paper about the tractor and decided to check it out, so we went to the man's house and looked over the tractor and equipment. The tractor was a 1965 International 424, and it came with a bush hog, potato plow, disk, turning plow, and an additional plow for laying out rows. Charley and the man discussed the tractor and the implements and decided on a fair price for it all. We had taken our 16' trailer with us to haul the tractor and equipment. (We bought the trailer the week before so that we would have it for hauling the tractor. Charley was that confident that he would buy a tractor, somewhere!)

We used the tractor to load a couple of the larger implements, and then we put the tractor toward the back of the trailer. By putting the tractor on the trailer last, we would be able to get the tractor off first, and then use the tractor to unload the implements. It was a wise decision.

We had decided that we would store the tractor and implements at Papaw's, because we had nowhere to store anything. We turned off Buffalo Road onto Gandy road. Charley stopped to make sure that everything was riding okay and had not come loose. We continued on Gandy Road, past Goody Fite's and started the trek up the steep hill.

Let me pause right here. Our truck was a 1992 GMC Sonoma, manual shift, no four-wheel drive and small engine. We had about 20,000 miles on the truck because we did not use the truck very often when we lived in Bowling Green. Charley had a company car, and I drove our car. The truck was nice to have when we needed to haul something, which was not very often.

Now on with the story…So, up the hill we went. Then the truck began to stall just before reaching the top of the hill, and could not pull over the hill with the load that we were hauling. Charley decided to back the truck and trailer, with the equipment on the trailer, down the hill to a flat spot just before the incline began to the hill. He did a great job keeping the trailer and truck in between the ten foot ditches all the while using the rear-view mirrors to keep him on track.

And then I just had to look in the rearview mirror to see how we were doing. Well, that broke Charley's concentration, and his view on where we were. So, Charley braked heavily waiting for his mirror view to return. Too late! The trailer and its load began to slide and drag us, truck and all, to the bottom of the hill. Did I mention that there was a curve at the bottom of that hill and just around that curve was a bridge – with no rails – over Brush Creek?

The trailer continued to drag us and the truck toward the curve, but with the Lord's help (I did a lot of praying during that hour-long, five-minute trip!), we rounded the curve backwards and the tractor and trailer began dragging the light pickup straight for the bridge…and water. Charley realized that the light truck was no match for the load that was in control, so he jack-knifed the pickup to give more traction against the motivated load that had us destined for an unavoidable doom.

I prayed hard, and Charley fought the truck – hard! We miraculously stopped at the edge of the road and bridge with only a few inches between us and the embankment that would have dropped us into the creek. We sat there for several moments to catch our breath – and breathe a prayer of THANKS – and then we got out of the truck.

After assessing the situation Charley decided to pull the trailer away from the embankment with me directing him. After he was able to get the trailer pulled away from the embankment, he unloaded the tractor and drove it over the hill. I followed with the truck and trailer with the implements. After we reached the top of the hill, Charley re-loaded the tractor, and we proceeded to Papaw's.

We told Papaw about our near mishap, and he suggested that we use his truck to go after the rest of the equipment. (His truck was a Ford F-150 with small engine and four-wheel drive.) So, we unloaded the tractor and equipment, unhooked the trailer from our truck, and hooked it to Papaw's truck, loaded the tractor and took off. We felt much safer in the larger truck.

We went back to get the rest of the equipment, again we used the tractor to load the equipment, and put the tractor toward the back of the trailer. We decided to go back to Papaw's by a different route (thank goodness there is more than one way to get in and out of that hollow!) so that we would not have to go back over the hill at Goody Fite's, just in case the bigger truck – with small engine – was also unable to clear that fateful hill!

The trip was uneventful until we started down a hill on Riverside Road. And then things really began to go crazy. As the truck and trailer bounced over the bumpy road going downhill, the weight of the tractor, which was on the back of the trailer behind the wheels, would raise the back wheels of the truck off the ground momentarily.

The downhill slope had a crooked pathway which made rounding the curves – and catching up with the bouncing back wheels – another challenging feat, even with the larger truck. We finally had to gear down the truck and stop using the brakes as the application of the brakes caused us to slide more. Finally, we were at the bottom of the hill and it was smooth sailing from that point forward. (*Note to ourselves: the next time we buy a truck, it will be a large truck with four-wheel drive and a heavy-duty engine!*)

May 2000…a year has passed since we first moved back to Tennessee. A lot has happened during this year. At times it seemed as though we were moving along quickly, only to look back and see that there was still a lot that needed to be accomplished…for us, that is!

Papaw told us several times that…"a garden waits for no man." He was right. The garden seemed to always need attention just at the time we needed to be working on the right-of-way or cabin. Of course, when the weather was good and we could have accomplished a lot on the power line right-of-way…well, the garden needed work, too. We had to choose which one we needed to do for the day…draw straws and the garden – and Papaw – always won.

Of course, we have never regretted our time spent with Papaw during those years of building the power line and the cabin…and gardening! And, we could never have done our projects without him, as his years of construction experience allowed us to do so much more than we could have done on our own. Even though his hair was as dark as Charley's, even at 80 years of age, it did not detract from the wisdom that lay beneath its roots – gray or dark!

The historical Columbia-Ashland Highway before the widening project began. Notice the banks and roots extending into the passage way, thus the need for widening.

The widened road in fore-front precedes the work being done by the dozer to get the same width throughout the roadway to the cabin.

Charley and Mr. Green looking at the work being done on the roadway to the cabin site.

CHAPTER 2

The Roadway
vs.
TWRA
(Tennessee Wildlife Resource Agency)

A s mentioned earlier, the old log road would need to be widened before we could get supplies through the woods and to our cabin site. Charley had spoken with TWRA earlier in the year to ascertain that there would be no problem with us widening the road to Papaw's property that crossed about one-half mile of the Laurel Hill Wildlife Reserve (LHWR).

Al Pollock, District Manager of Laurel Hill Wildlife Reserve (a division of TWRA), came down to review the proposed changes as laid out by survey tape along either side of the narrow roadway. He seemed to think every-thing would be okay and that he saw no problem with what we were proposing, but he would verify that with headquarters.

On June 21, 1999, there was a meeting with several TWRA officials, and it was decided that we should "buy" the easement. Al Pollock tried to call us on June 23, but was unable to reach us, so he left a message. On Friday, June 25, Charley tried to call Al, but could not reach him. Al finally reached us on Monday, June 28, to tell us there was a problem. It seemed that TWRA had decided that we would need to purchase the easement that we needed across the TWRA property. Before we could begin the process, an appraiser would need to appraise the property; a surveyor would need to do a survey; and an attorney would need to write up a deed and record such deed, all at our expense, of course. This total cost would be between $3000 and $5000, and probably toward the higher number.

Charley tried to call John Gregory, a name referenced by Papaw from his many years of association with TWRA at a higher level of management. Finally, Charley was able to speak to Steve Patrick ,who was John Gregory's supervisor. Charley requested a meeting for Papaw, himself, and me to go to Nashville to meet with John and Steve. Steve Patrick left us a message on July 5 that we would meet at 10:00 a.m. on Monday, July 12.

Charley spoke with Mr. Freeman, an Attorney in Lawrenceburg that Papaw had used for deeds. He also talked with Tim Underwood, a Pulaski attorney at Andrew Hoover's office where my sister, Pat, worked. Charley asked them about a prescriptive easement, having had many dealings with such during his many years of electric utility experience. Both attorneys confirmed that a prescriptive easement could be granted after seven years' use with no objections from the land owners. They also said squatters' rights (ownership) could be granted after 21 years of use with no objections.

On Sunday, July 11, Charley looked on the internet for cases on prescriptive easement lawsuits. He found six cases and all cases had been won in court, except for one case where a man had not used the property for 30 years, and then decided to begin reusing the easement.

It was agreed that Papaw would meet us at the trailer on Monday, July 12, about seven thirty. He showed up at 6:35 a.m. *(as an early riser he was always early wherever he went. He was always at church at least one hour before each service.)* We left by 7:15 and stopped at McDonald's in Columbia for breakfast.

We had gotten directions to the TWRA office from Steve Patrick's secretary. However, Papaw knew a better way. We would have been lost without him as the directions that we were given were not very clear. We arrived at TWRA about 9:20 a.m., our appointment being for ten o'clock. After a short wait, the three of us met with Steve Patrick and John Gregory in one of their conference rooms. Charley and Papaw explained that Papaw had used the property for about 55 years and that there had never been a problem with any prior owners of the property...or with TWRA, with using the road. Charley talked about prescriptive easements and the cases he found on the internet, along with his utility experiences with the same. Charley also relayed the information he had obtained from the two local attorneys, assuring Steve and John that we were not trying to claim squatters' rights as the justifiable owners to the property, but were merely seeking easement rights to maintain a 20-foot easement for clear passage through the property.

Papaw mentioned several prominent TWRA officials that he had dealt with over the years, (including fishing with some of them at Laurel Hill Lake) long years before the tenure of Steve and John. After about an hour, Steve told us that they would discuss everything with their in-house attorney and get back with us.

On Tuesday, July 13, John Gregory left a message on our phone that said we were to go ahead with the road widening, and TWRA would take care of the paperwork. TWRA surveyors would do the calls and survey, which would not cost us anything. We would need to pay a $500 fee to cover the cost of recording the survey with a federal agency in Atlanta where TWRA records are kept. Also there would be a fee of approximately $100 to prepare and record the easement document, locally. *(Final charges, however, were only for the easement recording and were under $100. All other charges were absorbed by TWRA. We were elated. And actually I think they were, too, since we did not claim squatters' rights on their property.)*

We have that message from John Gregory, along with others, recorded on a cassette to verify our correspondence and agreement with TWRA. Charley also had to send a letter explaining how wide and long an easement he would need. This was done and Charley and Papaw both signed the letter, and mailed it on July 16. The agreement was that the state's surveyor was to survey the easement after the road was completed to final grade.

Al Pollock looked at the road on July 15 and said that we could "take whatever we needed for a proper easement." Charley and Papaw told him that they would need a total easement width of only 20 feet. Al confirmed that that would be agreeable with TWRA and LHWR. With his approval, we could continue with our road-widening project.

On Monday, August 9, 1999, "the dream" began to take shape into reality. Larry Green, a dozer operator from Hohenwald, started the road-widening project to our proposed cabin site. He arrived at 7:45 am and stopped at three o'clock. A lot was accomplished during those few hours.

Let me pause right here and share a very important detail. There was no cellphone service in this area (and still isn't today). There are only two places where we could make or receive calls: one was at the cable at the beginning of the road (a higher elevation) and the other was at a peak in the road just before going downhill into the bottom. If we needed to get in contact with someone, it had to be done before we left the trailer, or we would drive to Papaw's and use his landline...or hit one of these two high spots with our cell phones. This inconvenience could be very frustrating...especially when we were expecting deliveries of supplies, and the drivers could not find us.

Now to resume the road-widening project, the weather of August 9 was in the 80s, and because there had been no rain since July 12, it was extremely dusty. After Mr. Green graded each section of the roadway, there was six to eight inches of dust in the road. It was almost like driving on snow. While he was bulldozing, there was so much dust that you could barely see his dozer. When he finished for the day, you could only see the whites of his eyes, because of the dust...turned mud...that had adhered to his sweaty body. But the road was beginning to look great.

After Monday's roadwork, Charley and Papaw gathered 275 ears of corn. We took that home with us, shucked and silked it, and went to bed. It was 10:30!

Charley and Mr. Green working on the roadway. Notice the thick dust on the roadway.

On Tuesday, we met Mr. Green at six-thirty. He widened the road up to the point where our driveway toward the cabin would begin. He then worked about 45 minutes on the driveway. He worked until three-thirty. It was another long, hot, dusty day with temperatures in the 90s. If the dust and heat were not enough, he also ran into two trees that had European hornets in them. Since these large pests can be very painful, he avoided these trees until he could spray and destroy their nests inside the knot holes.

Wednesday found us again meeting Mr. Green at six-thirty. *(Note: Charley was (and is) not an early riser, so meeting Mr. Green at 6:30 a.m. each morning was unheard of in Charley's world. In fact, his alarm does not register a 6:00 a.m. wake-up call – or not one that he could hear – but he hung in there like a trooper.)*

Mr. Green finished bulldozing the driveway, created a circle around the trees in front of where the cabin would be situated, and also cleared the spot for the cabin. Charley stayed all day with Mr. Green while I stayed at Papaw's, cooked lunch for him, and then took Charley something to eat. Mr. Green always brought his own lunch.

On Thursday, August 12, we again met Mr. Green at six-thirty.   He worked on the continuation of the Old Columbia-Ashland Highway from the spot of our tapped driveway toward our field in the bottom. He had to build up the road and hill as it dropped off to the bottom. He finished the road by 12:30 and it looked great.

Charley and I then went to Papaw's where Connie had fixed lunch for all of us. What an unexpected treat! We were accustomed to eating what we could find. Having a fully-cooked meal was wonderful!

After lunch we went home, peeled and sliced the apples for the freezer, and went to bed at ten o'clock. The weather was in the upper 90s for the day and there was still no rain since July 12. *(Even though this was a long, tiring four days, it was great to see so much accomplished. Mr. Green told us to let it rain, stay off the road a few days afterward, then have a grader go over it to make the ditches and put a slight hump in the middle, so the water would run off and not make ruts in the road. We would also need to put chert on the road and, especially, the hills and the driveway.)*

On Friday, September 3, 1999, Charley and I worked along the driveway cutting limbs on trees that were too low for large trucks to go under. Then we did some clearing in the thicket in front of where the cabin would be located. We also cleared some brush around the two springs. It was another hot and muggy day with temperatures in the upper 90s. In fact, it was so hot that we only worked two or three hours. Our bodies had not gotten accustomed to the heat after so many years of working in air conditioning.

On Wednesday, September 8, there were scattered showers today. It actually rained where we lived but NOT at the cabin site. It has not rained there for a couple of months and we cannot finish the road until we get rain.

To summarize our road work that did not make my journals, we finally got a good soaking rain around mid-October and it was sufficient to resolve the dust issue on our road. Earlier, we had contacted Johnny Finerty of Hohenwald to be ready for grader and chert work on the roadway whenever sufficient rain released him for such work. Johnny was prompt in getting the work done for us. He somehow could rationalize that one of the hillsides along the roadway would contain chert. He was right...a rich, red chert that packed almost to the surface texture of pavement. All went well with his loading of the dump truck and easing from the chert pit to the road-way above...until his last load. He needed a little more than his normal load to finish the last spot of the cherting process, but it turned out to be a costly decision for him. As he eased out of the pit with the overloaded truck, the rear axle of his dump truck snapped. Needless to say, that load never made it to the roadway. It had to be dumped and the truck towed to Hohenwald for repairs.

After smoothing the chert with the grader, and creating the slight rise down the center of the roadway, Charley then used his tractor to pull Johnny's crow's-foot packer to create the hard-surfaced roadway that gleamed with perfection.

Finally, after completing the roadway and TWRA finalizing their survey of our easement, it was Wednesday, July 26, 2000, when we went to Lawrenceburg to record the easement from TWRA, their portion of the roadway being in Lawrence County.

It took exactly one year to get the easement from the State. While we were appreciative of getting the easement at minimal cost to us, it made us very uneasy until it was recorded. It is amazing how long paperwork can take, especially when working with government offices. However, the people that we dealt with along the way were very courteous and helpful. We really appreciated the fact that although the paperwork was delayed, they did not insist at all on delaying our work that was ongoing throughout the year.

Mission One accomplished! The road was finished, now to start cutting the trees for the right-of-way for the power line and build our cabin.

Mr. Green working through a maze of trees to widen our road through layers of dust.

Chapter 3
The Cabin

It's Friday, November 5, 1999, and we have been very busy preparing the spot for the cabin and getting the easements for the power line. We burned the brush piles so that we would have the burning completed prior to starting the building of our cabin. After dark we used the fire from the brush pile to roast hot dogs and make S'mores. It was a beautiful and romantic evening. Well, except that Sully (our Maltipoo) did not appreciate the howling of the coyotes on the nearby hillside. He cowered under my chair afraid that the coyotes would make S'mores out of him. Even though we were amused by his reaction, Pat's little toy poodle, Little Mister, was later eaten by coyotes. Pat had let him out one morning to do his business as usual, and after he did not return in short order, she began looking for him...and the rest we will leave to your imagination – but it was verified as Little Mister. Little Mister was Sully's favorite playmate as they spent a lot of time together.

During the past several weeks we have manually dug the footers for the cabin. We hired someone to help us, and we paid him $6 per hour *(which he insisted on being paid at the end of each day)*. He eventually became unreliable, so, after a short period of time, we sought more reliable help. Ricky Houser, the young man who lived across from us on Smith Road, agreed to lay the blocks for the cabin at $1.25 per block.

We have worked long hours and days to get the footers aligned properly, so as to determine how deep to dig the footers for the concrete. We could not have gotten the job done if we had not hired some outside help.

The lot for the cabin looked fairly level before we started laying out corners and putting a level on the pull lines. The front near the garage door entrance was about two feet above ground, but the back corner was over eight feet above ground to where the cabin floor would level out. The cost of the gravel was too great to fill in the entire blocked-in area before pouring concrete for the floor of the cabin, so we decided to put chert in the area, pack it down and then put a load of gravel, a plastic moisture barrier, and steel wire for reinforcement, on top of the chert before finally pouring the concrete floor.

We have ordered the materials to start the building, and they should be delivered next week. Things move slowly, and then quickly…it is always hurry up and wait. We are either extremely busy or we are waiting for something to do. Ricky Houser and our hired man laid the blocks for the foundation. Johnny Finerty filled the foundation with chert that he took from our property. This was all done on Monday, November 8.

While using the backhoe to spread and pack the chert in the foundation, our hired hand got too close to the back wall and it began to pull away. We had to work on

Tuesday to tear down the wall and move some of the chert out of the foundation. Then Ricky re-built the wall on Thursday. He told us to wait at least a week before we poured the concrete floor. This was a delay that we did not expect, and extra cost that we could not afford, but we had to keep moving forward.

The representative from the health department came to "spot" the location for the septic tank and test our spring water.

Our son Greg's 30th birthday was on Saturday, November 13. That day we moved things around and laid block and boards to put the framing material on when it was delivered.

Note: we usually took our lunch – soup, chili, beef stew, etc. and would heat it on a small Coleman propane cooker. After each meal, I would take the pot to the nearby branch to wash it out. So, even in the woods I had to do the dishes.

The lunch break was usually the only break we took during the day. That was why we needed to take a day off here and there. (As mentioned in the previous chapter, our house in Bowling Green still had not sold.) Our finances were depleting quickly because we had pur-chased the materials for the cabin which are to be delivered on Monday.

Charley and I worked for a week to get the dirt and gravel prepared before the concrete was poured. We bent rebar and inserted it into the block and extended it to the reinforcement screening to be sure the wall did not kick out a second time.

On Friday, before the concrete was delivered on Monday, James Tolle came in with a bobcat and filled the back wall with gravel. Last week Charley had seen the bobcat along Waynesboro Highway. He stopped, found out who owned the bobcat, and then talked to Mr. Tolle about doing the work for us. It would have taken us days to manually fill the blocks with gravel…one bucket at a time. (Especially since I was doing most of the rock filling [another muscle-building project] while Charley worked on other projects.) When I heard Mr. Tolle coming down the driveway with his bobcat, I literally jumped up and down and yelled "Hallelujah!"

Charley told me to move the truck, which was parked in front of the foundation, so that Mr. Tolle could get in with the bobcat. In my excitement, I jumped in the truck, started it, took off the emergency brake and gave it the gas. Needless to say the gear was in reverse – I went backward into the block wall!

In my excitement I had forgotten to shift into first gear. I was shocked! I just knew that I had knocked down the front wall (we had just gotten the back wall re-built). Charley was very gracious because he said he knew it was an accident. He also said that the look on my face showed that I was sorry (and embarrassed). Just one more blonde moment to add to the list. I just knew that there was going to be another long, costly delay.

Thankfully, the wall was okay. Even though it is funny now, it was not so funny at the time.

The concrete for the floor was poured on Monday, November 22. It took 23½ yards of concrete. Papaw, Greg, Charley, our hired hand, and I were all the help that we had for this project. The first load of concrete was delivered by 10:30 a.m. and the last load was delivered about two o'clock. We had rented some long handled aluminum floaters to smooth the floor, and they worked great! We worked all day with only a short break and some "not-from-the-can" homemade vegetable beef soup. Everyone enjoyed the soup and the break. The concrete looked great when it was finished!

On Tuesday, after the concrete was poured, Charley went back to the cabin site to take up the skreed boards, but he could not remove them because the concrete was not fully cured.

Thanksgiving Day was spent at Papaw's. There were 35 to 40 people for lunch. There was so much food that everyone was sufficiently stuffed for the day. It was great to see everyone and to take a day off from working on the cabin.

After the long weekend we took off the 2 x 4 concrete forming (screed boards) and we put up a 2 x 6 form around the concrete pad for aligning the bottom edge of the framing of the building walls.

It's Friday, December 3, 1999, and the framework is up! Charley, Papaw, and I started the actual framing on

Tuesday. (Let me pause right here: Any morning when Charley, Papaw, and I met to start work, the guys would sit down and discuss the day's plans. They would talk for about 45 minutes or so while I was trying to hurry them along to get them started. I felt as though we were "wasting" time while we were sitting and talking. I learned that the "sitting and talking" was necessary to prevent having to do some jobs more than once. In my blonde way of "rushing things," I learned several times that the results can be costly with a project of this magnitude.) We worked about one-half day on Wednesday and completed the framing on Thursday. We worked hard but it was the kind of work that was not so exhausting. The framing looked great!

Charley and Papaw planning the next step.

Today we are making preparations to start raising the trusses. The temperatures for the week have varied from the 30s to the 60s, which was great weather for working.

Note: We did not have pneumatic air guns and tools (nor did we realize the ease of working with those types of tools) for building the walls or installing the trim work of our cabin. We used the old-fashioned hammer and nail...our only power tools were the cordless drill and electric saws (generator). Of course, using the ol' hammer and nail technique helped keep our muscles built up...but it sure played havoc with Charley's thumbnails! I surprised Charley (and myself) when I was able to hang on to the beams and hammer away to align the trusses. Oh, have I mentioned that I am afraid of heights? No time for fear...especially when you're on top of a ladder.

Papaw building a wall as he had always wanted to do. His smile shows how much he enjoyed working with us.

On Monday, Papaw, Bud, Charley and I put up the trusses. There were twenty-one 33-foot trusses in all. It was an exhausting day, especially for Charley.

On each end of the cabin and in the center we had installed a 16-foot 6 x 6 timber for stabilizing the trusses against wind shear. These timbers were anchored firmly to the 23 ½ yards of concrete in the floor and they were also anchored to the wall framing at these three locations. On each end at the top of the timbers we added an 8-foot 4 x 4 timber for temporary additional height for getting the trusses above the top plate of the side walls. An eye bolt and pulley were attached to the top of the 4 x 4 and a rope through the pulley attached to each truss below. The other end of the rope angled downward to the far end of the cabin where Papaw and I hoisted the trusses (with a double-pulley) up to Charley and Bud who lifted each end over the side walls.

One-half of the trusses were raised to each end of the cabin and then moved and spaced to their approximate location – securing these together with 2 x 4s until each could be precisely placed and secured at its exact location. *(As any good builder knows, a blueprint location and a "field" location can often vary by a few inches.)*

As with most big projects, we had one slight accident today. Charley hit himself in the forehead with the hammer when he was nailing down one of the trusses. He was on top of a fourteen foot ladder, but fortunately the whack to his head did not knock him out. A goose-egg sized lump formed quickly, but we applied cold cloths and he appeared to be okay. No time to stop and evaluate our injuries…work had to be done!

On Saturday, Pat, Jerry, Bud, Papaw, Charley, and I started the metal siding. The guys finished one end and put two sheets on the other end. Each piece had to be put up, marked for doors and windows, taken down, cut, put back up, and then screwed in place. It was a lot of work, but with everyone's help it went very smoothly.

Pat and Jerry brought chicken and biscuits from McDonald's for breakfast and also brought the makings for sandwiches and chips, cookies and drinks for lunch. It was delicious and it helped to not to have to pack lunch for everyone. December 23, 1999, Bud, Papaw, Charley and I finished the siding for the final end of the cabin (six pieces).

Papaw, inside, Jerry and Bud on the ground, and Charley on the roof put up the first piece of siding. This project went quickly with all of our good help.

We then installed the metal roofing. All of this was done in one day. I think Bud was surprised that we had gotten both sides completed by ourselves prior to today. We were all surprised that we were able to finish! We started about 8:15 a.m. and worked until about 5:15 p.m.,

while only taking only about thirty minutes for lunch.
(Yep, you guessed it! Canned soup heated on the propane
burner again.)

The roof has the crown work finished. Bud and Charley worked on Christmas Day to put the cap cover on the
roof. They worked another day to put the trim on the wall
corners and the edges of the roof.

On Tuesday, January 4, 2000, Charley and I rented a
U-Haul truck, and along with a hired helper, went to
Bowling Green to get our furniture and other things out
of the storage units. We were able to get everything from
the storage units onto the truck. However, we were
unable to get our things from the attic and the storage
building at the house due to lack of room on the truck, so
we will need to make another trip at a later time.
(Retrieving our things from the storage units gave us
more money to use toward our projects.)

Bud and Papaw helped Charley and me to unload the
truck on Wednesday, which took about two hours. The
unloading went so much faster than the loading (we did
not have to be so precise where we stacked each piece or
box). We put everything in the apartment side until the
shelves are built in the storage side. Then we will move
everything to the shelves of the storage side.

On Monday, January 10, the shelves were completed,
but on Tuesday we worked on the right-of-way for the
electric lines as the weather was unseasonably warm with
upper 50s to mid-60s. We wanted to take advantage of

the warm weather, so we will move boxes to the storage shelves when it is raining or extremely cold. Papaw came up and looked at the shelves, and he thought that they looked really good. I think that he was impressed with Charley's handiwork.

Monday, February 14, all of our boxes are on the shelves and in the attic. The framework for the bathroom, the utility closet, and the clothes closet, has been completed. We just lack the braces across the top of the bathroom and utility closet. Our next indoor project will be plumbing and wiring. Of course, the waste lines and the water line from the pump were installed in the concrete pad as the floor was poured. (*Happy Valentine's Day, Sweetie! No time for romance today!*)

Tuesday, February 15, we went to Lawrenceburg and bought a 550 gallon round tank for water storage. I worked on moving and storing boxes and Charley worked on finding the right spot for the tank. The man that was supposed to dig the hole for our septic tank had put us off several times. At first he said it was too wet, and then he had someone ahead of us. We had hoped to get the septic tank installed last week.

Tuesday, February 22, we had two propane gas heaters and a tank installed at the cabin earlier in the month. It was so nice to have real heat to back up to instead of a small unit on top of a 20 pound propane tank.

We have flowers blooming that we planted in November. Spring could not be too far away, or so I kept telling myself.   It seemed as though winter was hanging on for some reason, but we could not stop work to wait for spring.

We finally got the septic tank installed. Of course, it cost more than was projected and our funds are just about depleted. But we have to keep going. With that project finished we could focus on the building and the power line right-of-way.

On rainy days we mudded on the sheet rock in the cabin. We were about halfway through by the end of May. It was a slow process, especially as we could not work on it consistently, as we were continually working on other projects.

Charley made a three foot by five foot wooden rolling scaffold with adjustable height T-braces on each end of the scaffold. This helped greatly with installing the sheet rock on the ten foot ceiling. It also helped with mudding and sanding of the higher spots of the sheet rock. A lot of the time I would roll the scaffold with Charley on it to the spot he needed. Because I am so short, I had to use a small stepladder on the scaffold so I could reach the ten-foot ceiling.

June, 2000, we continued to work on the mudding on the cabin, and we are almost finished. We hope to paint as soon as possible. But gardening time is here so we cannot set a time to do any of our work.

The first two weeks of November we finished sanding the cabin, finished cutting out holes for the ceiling lights, and began painting the ceiling. Charley also got the wire set up to start pulling the power line on Wednesday, November 15. He had a very productive day. (More information on the power line in Chapter 4.)

Friday, November 17, 2000, we are back to work at the cabin. Charley and Bud finished painting the ceiling and then stomped the mud on the ceiling so that it will have a nice texture to it. The ceiling looked great...the guys did a fantastic job.

On Monday, November 20, 2000, we finished sanding the splattered walls where Charley and Bud had stomped the ceiling. It took several hours to finish the remaining sanding and then sweep up the floors. After we cleaned up from the sanding, I painted the bathroom and Charley went to pull up (sag) the rest of the conductors on the power line. When he finished pulling the wire, he came back to the cabin and painted the bathroom trim for me. The bathroom looked very nice. It took almost a gallon of paint for this one small bath. Charley put a second coat of paint on the bathroom walls on Tuesday and also painted the utility room and the kitchen areas.

On Wednesday, Charley finished painting the walls, with the trim work around the ceiling being the only remaining paint project.

Thanksgiving Day 2000: Charley finished painting the trim at the cabin while I was at Papaw's helping to prepare Thanksgiving lunch. He did a great job with painting the trim. Bit by bit things are getting done in the cabin.

On Friday, Charley installed some electrical switches and outlets at the cabin, but it began to rain and storm so much that it was too dark in the cabin to see well. That's just one more reason why we need to get electricity into the cabin...so we can see what we are doing.

On Saturday, December 30, 2000, Charley was at the cabin putting on light switch and outlet covers. I stayed home to put everything back in order from the Christmas holidays, and from the grandchildren being with us.

On Tuesday, January 2, 2001, we both worked at the cabin. YAY! Charley finished putting on the electrical outlets and cover plates. He put up the light fixtures in the bathroom, closet, utility closet, and made preparations for the kitchen light fixture. He also installed the medicine cabinet in the bathroom. Now all we need is electricity! Today's high temperature was 26° with a low of 8°. It was very cold outside but the cabin was cozy with the propane heaters.

On Friday, January 5, Charley got the ceiling fan up. He also put sheetrock putty around the outlets that had gaps around them.

On Wednesday, January 10, Charley got the truck fixed. We then went to the cabin and dug twelve post holes for his pole barn. It was hard to believe that we got all that done in one day...no chipping rock for those holes!

On Thursday, we did not accomplish very much. It was sleeting when we got up but we went to the cabin and Charley re-mudded around the outlets. When that dried we sanded and painted the spots. We then went to Papaw's and fixed lunch, made up his bed, folded his clothes and cleaned his kitchen.

Friday, we went to Lowe's to get materials for trimming out the doors and windows. While Charley shopped for the materials that we went for, I went to the clearance aisle and found a Sharp carousel microwave for $150 that was normally priced at $299. It had a vent and hood for over the stove built into the microwave. I loved the clearance aisle at Lowe's because you could find some really outstanding deals. The employees began to recognize me because I spent so much time on that clearance aisle, and they would let me know when they had some good deals.

On Monday, January 15, Charley took a load of wood to Bicycle Bob that he (Charley) had purchased. It was nearly noon before he got back home. *(Bicycle Bob was a northerner who moved south, bought a remote piece of property, and built a rough one-room shack out of discarded pieces of lumber and small saplings. His insulation was cardboard that he had collected from grocery stores, and his heat was a wood heater that fed a pipe through the wall. No water, plumbing, or electricity...how he has survived is still a mystery...but he was at our last book signing in Hohenwald in June, 2013. He attended our church [in Lawrence County]) with some of his neighbors on occasion. Everyone called him "Bicycle Bob" because he rode a bicycle everywhere he went.)*

When Charley returned home, we went to the cabin, and he got the anchors put in for two poles. Charley also cut down a few trees before the chain broke on the chain saw, so now we have to get that fixed. Just one more delay (and unexpected expense) of the overall process!

On Tuesday, after we realized that it was too cold to work on the power line, we went to the cabin and got some of the trim work cut out so we can put it up later.

While we were at the cabin I looked for silver trays and candlesticks for the Sweetheart Banquet that we are having at church on February 3 (read more about this event in Chapter 7). I looked a long time before I found the trays. I could not found the candelabra. Again, it was so frustrating to look for things and not be able to find them. Oh well, I will look for them another day.

We worked at the cabin on Friday. Charley put up the door between the kitchen and the storage area and put insulation in the cracks around the doors and windows, which should help the cabin side of the building stay a lot warmer. I chipped concrete all day. We had to chip the concrete floor so we can smooth out the rough places for carpet and padding. It was a very tedious job and I did not like doing it, but it had to be done. Even though I wore gloves most of the time, I still had bruised fingers and knuckles, and broken finger nails from hitting them so much with the hammer because I kept missing the chisel!

Thursday, January 25, 2001 found a high temperature of 39°. We worked at the cabin where we finished putting the stain on the beam. What a difference a coat of stain made. Even though the temperature was cold outside, the cabin was very cozy. Charley finished out the closet door, except for painting, and I chipped concrete again. It was a very slow job. We were tired and cold after a long day, but maybe a good hot bath will get both of us warmed up.

On Thursday, February 15, Charley met Ricky Houser at the cabin and agreed to let Ricky build the block foundation around our water tank. It will cost us more money, but the job will be done quicker if Ricky does it for us. Charley had enough to do without adding that job to his list.

On Saturday, March 3, Pat and Jerry came to help us! Having two more people helped us get a lot accomplished. Charley and Jerry went to the pole where the meter will be installed. They got the conduit, meter base and the breaker box installed and almost finished before they were rained out. Pat and I cleaned out the trench for the water line, except for about six feet that had not been broken up, before we were rained out. Pat said, "I don't see how you have done this day, after day, after day. I would be worn out!" I said, "I *AM* worn out, but I have to keep working if we are going to get the job done."

Charley patched the rough spots in the concrete floor after Pat, Jerry, and I cleaned out the living area. When we took the plastic off the appliances, the cabin looked so much brighter without plastic covering everything.

On Monday, March 5, I worked at the cabin. I mopped and painted the floor, painted the trim work around the doors and windows, and painted the trim around the cubby hole (space for towel storage). I plan to finish the inside of the cubby hole later.

On Thursday, I finished caulking most of the doors and windows. I wiped down the walls to get the dust off, painted some trim work, moved boxes and sorted some boxes for putting in the attic. I also raked the leaves from around the front of the cabin. I am exhausted. *While I was working at the cabin, Charley worked on the survey for Papaw's property. (See Chapter 5.)*

Friday, Charley put up the trim that I painted yesterday. Then he put the door knob on the bathroom door, and finished installing the chandelier in the dining area. He also helped me move some boxes around in the attic so we could put additional boxes up there.

On Saturday, Pat came over and helped us move some boxes from the trailer to the cabin. We would not have made it without her. She brought Jerry's truck, and with our truck, we were able to make a lot of progress toward our eventual move. I need to point out that we had stored a lot of boxes in the extra two bedrooms at the trailer – things that we did not want to put in storage.

The trench for the water line had filled in during the rain over the past weekend so Pat and I cleaned it out...AGAIN! We started on the trench for the electric line, but Charley needed us to help him pull wire through the conduit. It turned out to be a horrendous procedure but after using pulleys and a hoist to get the wire through the conduit on the inside of the cabin, we were so pleased to get it done. But when we went outside – well, the wire had pulled back out. Charley spent close to another hour on it, but could not get it finished. Pat and Jerry came back over after church on Sunday, and Charley and Jerry finished the remaining wire pulling into the main panel. They also got the conduit on the transformer pole, but we need more wire to go in this conduit. Hopefully, Charley and I can get the rest of the wire in the pole conduit without any problems.

Pat and I did get the water pipe in from the cabin to the beginning of the downward slope to the spring house. Pat said she was not leaving until it was done. She was **NOT** digging that trench again! So, we got it done. We were all relieved to see the water pipe in the ground even if it was not completely covered.

Charley smashed his finger with a hammer, and although it looked rough, it did not appear be broken. He said that it did not hurt...too much. I think that by now he was accustomed to having smashed fingers!

On Wednesday, March 14, Charley and I worked on the breaker box inside the cabin terminating the large service wires. Afterward, Charley worked on installing the lines in the conduit on the pole, while I worked on finishing the ditch for our remaining waterline down to the pump house. (With all this digging and moving boxes I have developed some serious muscles. Not bad for a 100+ pounder!)

Papaw and Charley looked over the areas of our property line between us and Jen (Charley's youngest sister). They also looked over the spots where Papaw hunts for turkey to see if there were any "scratchings". Turkey season starts March 31.

It's Sunday, March 18. Today between the morning and evening church services, Charley put up the trim on the beam and the kitchen window. He also put the light switch and electrical outlets in the storage area. I caulked the kitchen window and the trim on the bathroom door. I also put some empty boxes in the van to use for additional packing at the trailer.

On Tuesday, March 20, we ordered our brick and block. The brick is for the bottom part of the cabin and the blocks are for the spring house building around the water storage tank. We went to Lowe's and bought an 18,000 BTU window air conditioner for $250 that we found on the dent line. The normal price for that unit was $427. Another great deal at Lowe's! We also went to Harris Carpet and picked out carpet for the cabin. We returned to the cabin and met with the lady from Harris

Carpet, so she could measure the floor space. It was a very busy day, but a lot of excitement to see so much progress being made.

Thursday, March 22, 2001, WE HAVE ELECTRICITY!! Ah, lights. Thank you, Lord, for electricity! The lights look fantastic! I kept turning them on and off just to see them work. It may have been a waste of electricity, but we have waited so long for this day that I could not stop myself. Charley stood there laughing as I ran from light switch to light switch trying the lights. Did I mention the dimmer switch on the chandelier? I kept dimming the lights and then raising them again. Charley finally told me to calm down.

Yes, I was very hyper over lights! You cannot appreciate the simple pleasure of electricity, until you have been without it so long...and, oh yes, installed the power line yourself. It sure makes you appreciate the linemen (and groundmen...blonde or not) who faithfully keep our power flowing.

We have also temporarily laid the water pipe down to the spring house. Weather permitting we hope to finish the pipe tomorrow. And we may even get to work on the springs as well. The next best thing to electricity is water, so we must get our water lines completed soon.

The carpet is scheduled to be installed next Wednesday. Our goal at this point is to move by next weekend.

The high today was 69° with a north wind and rain. It was a nice day until about three o'clock when it began to rain and the temperature started dropping. It is now in the 40s.

Charley called Ricky Houser on Friday morning and Ricky went down to the cabin and started the block building around the water storage tank. Charley and Ricky had to carry the block down to the pump house site (about 100 feet). It was a very slow process as they could only carry a couple of blocks each. It took many trips to get the block down to the site. Ricky began to lay the blocks...quickly, and by the end of the day the job was completed. His workmanship was outstanding! They also cleaned out the springs and bricked around them. Ricky seemed to enjoy being around Charley. They made a good team...both perfectionists! As the blonde apprentice, it was hard for me to feel as though I "measured up" to their expectations, but they were very patient with me.

I went to Papaw's and fixed lunch for all of us: Charley, Ricky, Papaw, Paul, and me. While I was there I made Papaw's bed and folded his clothes.

On Saturday I put another coat of stain on the beam, and then I went to Papaw's to help Sandy cook lunch for the four of us. I have been packing up the kitchen at the trailer. I have gotten quite a bit packed up, and now we are just waiting to move.

On Sunday, March 25, Charley and Ricky finished cleaning out the springs and put plastic over them to keep leaves and other "things" from falling into the water. They put Clorox in the springs and the storage tank to purify the water. They also finished tying the two springs together and have the pipe down to the water tank. And then they put pipe around the inside of the spring house to an overflow pipe that extended through the far wall.

Charley estimated that it would take 20 hours to fill up the tank before it would begin to overflow. Twenty hours would be at 1:15 p.m. on Monday. The overflow actually began to run at 1:17 p.m. How is that for accurate calculations? Only an engineer could do that!! It was very exciting to see the water start flowing. And, yes, we were watching the very instant the water started running out the overflow pipe. I was almost as hyper at seeing the water run as I was with the lights turning on and off. Now to get the final touches on everything so we can have water in the cabin.

The brick work was beautiful. Ricky finished the front of the cabin on Monday and it was amazing what a difference the brick made. Our building was beginning to look like a house.

Charley worked on the commode on Monday, March 25. He had to chip out and put an offset in because the hole was too far from the wall. He hopes to get it finished on Tuesday. No more using the bathroom in the woods!! Do you know how painful it is to sit on a log, not to mention all the no-see-ums that await you? (See Definitions.)

Ricky finished the brick around the front and side of the building on Tuesday. It now has the appearance of a real house and feels like a real house, too, with lights, and water not far away.

On Wednesday Charley got the pump put in and the pipe glued all the way to the spring house. He also got the commode put in but he lacked one piece and that was in the van. (Of course, we were in the truck today.) He also pumped out part of the water out of the water tank and siphoned out all of the trash floating on top of the water. The water is so sparkling clear that it almost glows.

The carpet was also installed today. Everything is coming together and our little cabin in the woods is beginning to look more like a home.

Charley finished the pump and spread out all the un-even dirt in the clearing where we hope to build a "real house" someday. He also fixed the bad bump in the branch crossing for the road going to the upper place. Later he plowed Papaw's garden for him.

I got the brick picked up from around the building and did some outside cleaning. Every little bit of cleaning makes a lot of difference.

On Thursday, March 29, 2001, we moved into the cabin! Thank you, Lord. One comical thing happened to-day…we blew the top element in the water heater. It was caused by the air in the pipes which stopped the water running into the tank and made us think that the water heater was full. Charley was too tired and too pressured to get moved in, so he failed to reason that the tank was not full. He failed to "bleed" the air out of the lines at the faucets. When we turned on the water heater the element blew out. It sounded like an explosion...well; it was an explosion, but a contained one. So, now we will have to get another element to replace the blown one. So we have water, and some hot water, but not as efficient as with dual elements. Oh well, as least we are civilized again!

Lizzie and Fluffy ran off into the woods as soon as we let them out of the cage, but we are sure they will be back in the morning. They are going to love their new home with all the trees and fresh air. Maybe they can help keep down the lizards, mice, and other critters that want to share our cabin space.

We moved one load of things today: beds, china cabinet, chest of drawers, recliners, washer and dryer, and several boxes. It is hard to believe that we could move so much by ourselves. We still need to move the big-screen TV, corner hutch, computer and accessories and all of our clothes and small items. I sure would like to finish tomorrow and get things cleaned up at the trailer.

As I write this at eleven o'clock here in our cabin, I am struck by the sound of the whippoorwill. This "invisible night hawk" keeps singing *whip-poor-will...whip-poor-will...whip-poor-will.* It is a beautiful, melodic, yet lonely, sound. (It reminds me of Charley's poem, *Lineman: Highest Profession.*) The sound takes me back to my childhood when we could hear the whippoorwill sing its song at night.

Then there is the darkness...there are no outside security lights so there is total darkness (no moon tonight!). Darkness so thick that you could cut it with a knife...if you could see how! With the darkness and the sounds of the whippoorwill there is an almost eerie feeling. It has been a very long time since we have lived in this type of atmosphere. I believe we are truly going to enjoy our new life in the country...once we get used to it again.

On Friday it rained. Greg came over to the cabin and stayed about four hours. We finally realized that he was going to be there for a while, so we went out to get some hamburgers to eat because we did not have any food at the cabin. Let me remind you that we are no longer at the trailer with a store and deli less than a mile away. The nearest "anything" in the way of food is ten plus miles away. Greg helped Charley put in our vanity while I went for burgers, so now the bathroom is complete. (Ha! Indoor plumbing in the woods!)

Later Charley and I went to Oaks Hardware to get the element for the water heater and other necessary pipe fittings for the kitchen sink, the dishwasher, garbage disposal, and the icemaker. Fortunately this hardware stays open until 11 o'clock each night.

On Saturday, March 31, we went back to the trailer to get the rest of our things but Stephanie (our landlord) came over and stayed about an hour. Then Jay, our neighbor, came over three times...so we lost another hour to an hour-and-a-half. He was moving into the trailer as we were moving out, so he is anxious to see us leave...but not so much so as to let us Git-R-Done! But he is going to miss all the home-cooked meals that we took to him on occasion.

We made it with all the furniture except the dining room table, an old TV and more boxes. We went back for a second load but it began to rain so we did not get finished with moving everything. I was overwhelmed at what we did not get finished with, and how much more we have to do. We still have things in cabinets and all the closets. There are boxes everywhere! I told Charley that I could not see how we could have accumulated so much stuff. (I honestly believe that the boxes were multiplying like rabbits when we were not looking!) We finally had to give up and come home – *to the cabin*. That has a nice ring to it...home to the cabin.

Connie and Sandy brought us BBQ sandwiches for supper. They are so thoughtful. I don't believe that I could have cooked anything. The temperature today was in the low 60s... not too bad, but it was windy. I hope April warms up some. We do not have TV at the cabin, so we do not know what the weather is going to be like from day-to-day. We are supposed to get our satellite installed on Tuesday. We will see!

We are overly tired tonight. We have overworked ourselves trying to get moved and settled into the cabin.

Hopefully we will get a good night's rest tonight. We set the clocks ahead one hour tonight as it is time to change from Central Standard Time (CST) to Central Daylight Time (CDT)...but we also lose an hour with daylight savings time – Lord help us! We made it to bed at 12:10 a.m. (CDT) – after setting our clocks ahead.

Monday, April 2, we got in bed about 11:30 last night (Sunday) and did not get up until 8:30 this morning. We definitely needed the rest...plus, we lost an hour of sleep on Saturday night due to Daylight Savings! Charley said he felt better. I believe he feels relief at being in the cabin. *(It was so nice to not have to get up, get dressed, and head out to the cabin...we were already there!)*

Today, Charley got the sink and garbage disposal installed. He fixed the dryer, cut off the closet and utility doors, and installed the dishwasher. It is amazing how much he has gotten done.

He temporarily used the orange counter top that we had when we lived in Bowling Green. It was in the house when we bought it, but we later replaced it with a nice, pretty blue counter top. I had hoped to never see that counter top again as it is not even a pretty counter top...but right now, it beats no counter top at all. Oh well, it will suffice until we find the color we want.

I went to the trailer and finished all the packing and cleaned up the bathrooms. It took me all day to finish, and I did not get home until 7:15. Then I had to go to

Oaks Hardware (twenty miles away) to get a part for the dishwasher.

I did some laundry and on the second load when the washer began to empty out it caused the commode to gurgle and water came up in the bathtub. Somehow the drain line is stopped up at the septic tank. Charley called the man who installed the septic tank and he is supposed to come by and check out the problem for us.

Also, we are supposed to get our DirecTV satellite system installed tomorrow (Tuesday) afternoon. I am not even sure we can get satellite in this remote location. And I do mean remote.

Lizzie and Fluffy showed up over the weekend. They were hungry and seemed glad to see us. We had been calling to them, but they would not come to us. I am sure they thought they had been thrown to the wolves…or coyotes!

On Tuesday, April 3, the man came and fixed our septic tank for us. He had to clean out the intake pipe (there was a flaw in the tank design). We also got the satellite installed. I am impressed! We have re-joined civilization. Now we can watch the Weather Channel every day!

I went back to the trailer today and got a few things, and cleaned out the refrigerator. We are absolutely over-flowing with "stuff!" I cooked supper tonight at our new home. We had fried chicken, green beans, corn, gravy, and biscuits. We took a plate of food to Papaw, and he really enjoyed the meal. It was so good to see him eat a good meal, since we had been so busy with the moving that we had not had time to cook for him (or us).

Now we are relaxing for a bit before we go to bed. It feels good to sit and watch TV for a while. Sully is pleased to be settled in, too, as he and I share the recliner. *(Note: we bought two Lazy Boy recliners for the cabin – Charley's was regular size and mine was jumbo sized for Sully and me…and he always claimed more than his half.*

It rained this Wednesday morning. It was a pleasant sound as it hit the tin roof. I was reminded of my early childhood while listening to the soothing sounds of the pinging rain.

We finished moving everything today. We unloaded the last load at 6:20, then ran in the cabin, changed our clothes, and left for church (which started at seven and was about eighteen miles away). The low this morning was in the 50s, and the high was in the upper 70s. I love spring!

On Friday, Charley built a shelving unit to go over the computer desk. *(The desk is actually a small desk with six drawers (three on each side) and a middle drawer. The desk was bought for my younger sister during the 70s. She sold the desk to me many years ago, and we continue to use it.)* The unit has so much storage space with all of the cubby holes designed to fit specific needs (i.e. printer, fax, paper, books, etc.).

On Tuesday, April 10, the temperature got up into the 90s today. It was about 85° inside the cabin. We have not installed the air conditioner, and we definitely need to get that done before the heat of summer...which appears to be here already! The surrounding trees make for nice shade, but they do not keep out all of the heat.

On Thursday, Charley installed the dishwasher and hooked up the ice maker. It was great to have both hooked up and ready to use. Especially the dishwasher. I don't mind cooking when I don't have to wash every dish by hand. (*There is no dishwasher at Papaw's so I have been doing a lot of dishes by hand these past couple of years*). We have the windows open and a fan blowing to get some of the hot air out of the cabin so we can sleep.

Monday, April 16, it seems as though we are always looking for things. The one-room concept is nice, but I sure hope that we can survive the cramped quarters. We had a four bedroom home in Bowling Green, and then moved to a three bedroom trailer – less two packed storage bedrooms – and now we are living in one large room. We don't seem to have room for anything. We have things stored under the beds and in the storage side. Sometimes things are not as convenient as we thought they would be. I know that it will take some time to adjust...but we will need to adjust soon! *Lord help us!*

On Wednesday, we went to Lowe's to get wallpaper and border for the kitchen. I really wanted a screen door for the door leading to the deck, but they did not have the one that I wanted in stock. We also got the towel racks and other accessories for the bathroom. Charley put up the border in the bathroom and started the wallpaper in the kitchen. Of course, I was on "stand-by" to get whatever tools he needed.

He went walking a little later and brought me a sweet bouquet of Dogwood blossoms, bush honeysuckles, and little red flowers. It was a beautiful bouquet.

Charley's shoulder was better on Friday (see Chapter 8), so he worked on the little storage building: leveled it up, patched holes, and fixed the doors. It was ready to be painted.

On Saturday, Charley cut all the shelving boards for the inside closet, and I painted the boards. After the boards dried he put them in the closet, and then I put our clothes on the rod and the shoes on the shelves. The closet worked great! But for a city girl's wardrobe a 2-foot by 6-foot closet – less a 2-foot folding door – which basically accommodated three changes of clothes. The rest of our clothes were stored in boxes and put in the storage side.

Charley put up two sets of shutters on the windows, fixed a window screen, and put up the Titanic dinner bell that he had given me for my birthday (in January). We both really worked hard today, and a lot was accomplished.

On Wednesday, April 25, we finished hanging the wallpaper and the border in the kitchen. The kitchen looks so nice. Charley put down the baseboards and I went through boxes to put in the storage building. I put all the boxes of jars in the storage building to use later for canning.

We brought the 4-wheeler home today (it was in the shop for repairs). Now I can use it to haul the boxes to the building. It will be a lot easier than using the wheel barrow...still building muscles!

On Monday, April 30, I painted the metal storage building. Charley put up our screen door. Now we can let fresh air in without the bugs! Of course you cannot live in the country without bugs. Papaw always said that a "screen is just something that mosquitoes use to push the gnats through." He believed that nothing could keep a gnat out, and he was right.

Tuesday, Charley built some shelves for the storage area beside the kitchen door. Now I can store small appliances and large cooking pots on the shelves and get them out of boxes. It will be so nice to not have to dig them out every time that I need to cook. I can just go to the shelf and get what I need. A-a-a-h-h, civilization in the woods!

On Thursday we moved all the concrete blocks (96 of them and, yes, I counted them) and the scrap metal and security light fixtures away from the building and over to where he plans to build a pole barn. Things are really beginning to look better around the cabin. I had told Charley that we were beginning to look like "rednecks" with all of the stuff just outside the front door…so I think that motivated him!

Saturday, May 5, Charley finished the gutters on the front of the cabin, and I cleaned out the refrigerator in the storage area. I was also on "stand-by" in case he needed anything. When I am on "stand-by" that means that I cannot venture far from where Charley is working (of course, you linemen know all about stand-by). If he needs me to get a tool for him he does not want to have to stop what he is doing to find me…therefore the need to be nearby when he is working on a project.

On Tuesday, May 15, we cooked lunch for Bud, Ola (his wife) and Papaw at our cabin. Bud and Papaw had helped us so much that we wanted to prepare a meal for them. Everyone seemed to enjoy the meal and our intimate, one-room setting.

On Thursday we went to the Mennonites and bought twelve quarts of strawberries. Charley helped me prepare them for the freezer except for enough to make two pies, some for eating, and some for putting over yellow cake. Of course, we shared with Papaw, and he enjoyed them as much as we did. The temperature inside the cabin got up to 85° today while I was using the washer, dryer and doing some cooking. It is really hard to work when it is that hot indoors. (Almost like being at Papaw's where I could get a tan while inside! See Chapter 5.)

Tuesday, May 29, I went through a few more boxes from the trailer. Amazing how much "stuff" we have accumulated these past sixteen years. The real question is: how much of this stuff do we really need, and why do we hang onto it? Of course, the day after we toss it, we need it!

On Monday, June 4, Charley worked on the frame for the air conditioner. I went to Papaw's and defrosted and cleaned out the freezer. I also cooked lunch for all of us.

And on Tuesday, we had air!! Thank you, Lord! It took most of the day, but Charley got it done. It sure feels much better. I don't know how much longer I could have taken the heat. We are definitely in civilization now! Oh, it sure feels good in the cabin now that we have air. We will sleep so much better tonight!

On Friday, Charley and I cut several small trees around the cabin in preparation of starting the deck. We got several cut up and moved but we have more trees that need to be cut down.

Of course, we could not do this job without some sort of mishap. Charley and I had tied off a tree so that it would not fall toward the cabin. It was my job to crank the come-along to tighten the rope and keep the tension on the cable so the tree would fall in the direction he wanted…toward me! Well, when I cranked the come-along, a rope broke. The tension was so tight, and I was pumping so hard, that I was thrown a complete flip and landed face up in the ditch that we had not completely filled in for the power line to the house.

I hit the ground so hard that I saw stars swirling around me, and the breath was completely knocked out of me. Sully came running and jumped up on my chest and started licking my face to make sure that I was all right. Charley thought the slow-motion flip could not have hurt me and started yelling, "GET UP!! THE TREE IS ABOUT TO FALL!" Well, of course, I could not get up.

Charley finally came over. He had to move Sully out of the way so he could get to me. I hurt all over...my head, my back, my neck. I felt as though the universe was spinning. I could smell the pungent aroma of the dirt as I was lying there trying to determine if anything was broken. But I got up! Charley reconnected the rope and re-tightened the tension, and we got that tree down – exactly where he wanted it to fall. The show must go on…even when you have mishaps.

It is Friday, June 22, and we have had a busy week. Charley has been working on bids for the materials for our deck. It is going to be rather expensive, but we will have the deck across the back and side of the cabin so it will be fairly large. It will be very nice when we are finished. We hope to screen in a section of the deck so that we will have an extra room for sitting and admiring the woods and its accompanying wildlife.

Charley did help Papaw mow his yard although the vibration from the mower made his neck hurt even more. Then we went to Huntsville for puppet training. It was a lot of fun, and we learned some very interesting techniques. Even though he was in pain he enjoyed the puppet training and also learned a few magic tricks, and how to make animal balloons.

On Wednesday, June 27, Lowes, from Florence, delivered our lumber for the deck. We are anxious to get started on yet another building project. Of course, the building of the deck will be done in our spare time. *(Note: It is always interesting to me that I always comment that we will do something in our spare time. The question is: "What spare time?")*

On Thursday, after we finished helping Papaw with the potatoes, we returned home, and it began to rain and storm (thank you, Lord that we got the potatoes in before it began to rain). The electricity went off for about an hour. Thank goodness it was the co-op's outage and not our own power line, so it came back on without Charley having to do any lineman troubleshooting.

Now when you install your own power line, you are responsible for fixing it when anything happens. If a tree falls on the line, you cannot call the power company to come fix it for you...you fix it yourself. So it was an anxious hour waiting to see if that electricity would come back on. We always called Papaw, and if his electricity was out, then it was the co-op and not our problem.

On Monday, July 2, 2001, We went to Lowe's and TSC in Columbia to get nails, screws, and other materials for building the deck. Charley got a saw (an early gift for his birthday) that he can use for cutting the boards.

On Tuesday, Charley and I moved more than 40 logs in the bottom (logs that had been left behind by the loggers), and then Charley and Papaw bush hogged until it became too stormy to work.

On Thursday, Charley worked on a tool shelf at the cabin and hung some peg board to put his tools on. It will be nice to be able to find things when we need them. Maybe we won't spend more time looking than fixing. But don't count on it. We have a knack for not putting things back where they belong…hence the need to look for things when we need them.

Friday, July 6, was Charley's 54th birthday, and he worked all day! He installed the corner posts for our deck. He had to dig the holes, line up the posts, brace them, and then mix up and pour concrete in each hole. Happy Birthday, Sweetie...but life goes on!

On Saturday, Charley and I worked on the deck. He capped off the cement around the deck posts so that the rain will run off and not soak into the poles. We have the outside frame up on the side of the cabin, and we need to finish it across the back. Then we will be able to start laying the floor. We did not get to work on the deck very long because it began to storm. We got quite a bit of rain along with wind, thunder, and lightning. The propane company delivered our gas today at $1.15 per gallon.

We should have enough to last us through the winter for our 600 square foot living area.

Monday, July 23, we came through the left side door today. Charley has the framework and floor on the deck past the window, but they are not fastened down. It sure looks good and it feels good to be able to walk around the cabin. We will not be confined to going in and out just the one door now...we will have three doors! That is a lot of doors for 600 square feet. We also picked blueberries today. We got about one-half gallon. We put some in the freezer, and we are going to make a cobbler with the rest.

I cleaned house and did laundry today, but that is about all. I haven't really done a lot, but I am tired. I think the lock-in with the youth from church, and the weekend are catching up to me. (See Chapter 7 for details.)

Saturday, July 28, Charley worked on the deck (and helped with canning) and he was able to lay most of the boards down but they are not yet fastened. It is going to look great when it is finished.

On Monday, August 13, Charley finished laying all the deck boards today and has most of them fastened down. What a difference this deck has made to our little cabin. Charley decided to go outside after dark to admire his handiwork by the light of the porch lights at each exit door. Well, he was walking barefoot on the carpet and just eased right onto the floor-level deck. He stood there a few minutes admiring the work, and then re-entered the cabin. A short time later he began gasping and could not get a good breath. He then realized that the fresh treatment on the wet deck (there was heavy dew after sundown) had entered the pores of his feet and was suffocating him. He washed his feet several times and then soaked them in some warm water. His breathing problem calmed down and he was soon back to normal.

He had read about the danger of the wood treatment for decking, but had forgotten, until it happened so quickly to him. As his breath was fading, he recalled the article he had read months earlier...thank the Good Lord that he recalled that article quickly!

On Thursday night, September 13, we had a thunderstorm to come through our area. We got about three hours of sleep. Lightning hit a tree behind the cabin which knocked out our water pump, telephone, and, of course, the satellite. So today I went to Papaw's and filled up buckets with water so that we could flush the commode. Charley had to replace the Ground Fault Interrupter (GFI) at the power pole and our pump began to run. Hallelujah! We have water again!!

The pump was still being fed from an extension cord laid across the ground from the breaker pole to the pump. This cord went right beside the tree that was struck by lightning. The extension cord had complete circles cut around the outer covering about every nine inches in perfectly spaced segments for the entire length of the cord. No internal wires of the cord were damaged. *(Note from Charley...In my 42 years of utility experience, I have never seen anything similar, before or since that incident!)*

On Saturday, we discovered that the lightning (on the 13th) really wreaked havoc on our little cabin. All of the GFIs had to be reset (we did not realize that we had so many). I opened the freezer today to find that the food was thawing. Charley reset the outlet, but it was not as easy as it should have been, but it did reset. At least the freezer is now working. (We worked too hard this summer putting vegetables and fruit in the freezer to lose these now! This is a large part of our winter's food supply.)

We dug a ditch and buried the gas line to the cabin. Charley also used the tractor and the potato plow to dig the line from the power pole to the spring house for our pump's power. I am going to try to finish cleaning it out next week while he is at work (oh, did I mention Charley has gone back to work...he really needed some rest! See Chapter 8). Connie and Sandy came by late on Saturday afternoon for about thirty minutes and brought us BBQ and the fixings along with some homemade banana pudding. Oh, was it nice to not to have to cook supper after digging ditches all day.

Well, during the last two weeks of September, we finally finished the underground wiring from the power pole to the pump, along with its required ditches. Since Charley was back at work, we hired Johnny Finerty to cover the ditches of our power lines and water lines from the spring house, just prior to having a winter freeze-up of our exposed water lines. The critical work at the cabin was done just in time to move to Sandy Hook…and begin a new chapter in our lives.

One interesting note about the cabin – after we moved to Sandy Hook where Charley worked with the Mount Pleasant Power System as General Manager, we had a visitor to our fair haven. It was an escaped convict from a Wayne County facility, who just happened upon our little cabin in the woods, and found it to be "just right" much like Little Goldilocks of *The Three Bears*. Well, everything was "just right" including the change of clothes that was swapped for his prison attire, the food and drink from the cupboard and refrigerator, and all other necessities of his secluded life.

But the chapter that was not included in *The Three Bears* was the one about Little Goldilocks running out of cigarettes. Well, this was a chapter of its own, "One More Reason to Not Smoke." Needless to say, the nearest store for cigarettes was at least five miles away, and the authorities had the area saturated. So as soon as our "boarder" hit one of the main roads, he was picked up.

We were contacted by authorities about our "visitor," and we were asked to allow them to search our cabin for any evidence left there. The prisoner had attempted to open one of our spare transformers to possibly get copper for selling to purchase his cigarettes, but he could not get the top off the tank. Fortunately we found nothing of value missing from our haven...since the only thing of real value there was the peace and serenity that saturated the place.

An early picture of the finished cabin before the full deck was built to the left side and across the back, and our small pickup.

Chapter 4
The Power Line

On Wednesday, September 8, 1999, Charley met with Mike Potts from the Meriwether Lewis Electric Cooperative (MLEC) so that they, MLEC, could see where we wanted to tap off with our electric lines from the MLEC primary line between Papaw and his neighbor, W. H. Bancroft. The approximate spot was located...and settled...or so we thought. *(However, a year or so later, with the right-of-way cut and several poles set, Charley called to have the engineer, Mike Potts, come back to do a final spotting of the MLEC meter pole. He found out that another engineer, a Mr. Skelton, would be his new contact person, so an appointment was made.*

Upon arrival, the MLEC District Manager, Johnny Driver, accompanied Mr. Skelton to the meeting. Mr. Driver was inquiring as to what qualifications Charley had that might allow him to install a primary power line from this spot to his cabin site. After about thirty minutes of discussion of where Charley had worked, and the many projects that he had engineered and implemented, Johnny concluded that if anyone was capable of installing their own power line that it would certainly be Charley. He told Charley to proceed with his power line and let MLEC know when we were ready for power hookup.)

On Saturday, September 11, Charley worked on the computer to prepare the easement for the power line. Papaw and Mr. Bancroft would each need to sign their respective easement across their property. After he finished work on the computer, we went walking for a while. The day was beautiful with temperatures in the upper 80s.

On Tuesday, January 11, 2000, we worked on clearing the right-of-way for the electric lines. The weather was unseasonably warm with upper 50s to mid-60s. We have tried to take advantage of the warm weather and work outside whenever possible.

On Tuesday, May 2, Charley and I worked on the right-of-way until noon. After lunch we went to Papaw's and helped him plant the garden.

Note: Before we dressed for the day, each morning I would take our clothes (jeans, shirts, socks,) out to the deck, turn them wrong-side out, spray them with an insect repellant, then lay them on the deck rails to dry. (If it was a cloudy morning, I would put the clothes in the clothes dryer to dry.) After our clothes were dry, I would turn them right side out and we would put them on. The purpose of this was to prevent being bitten by ticks, no-see-ums, chiggers and any other biting insects. After performing this procedure for many months, we found out that spraying our clothes with the insect repellant could cause breathing problems, and other health issues due to the prolonged absorbing of the insect repellant through our skin pores. Just another example that the Good Lord took care of us when we did things that were not too smart!

It's Tuesday May 9, and another week has passed by, filled with so much to do. We have worked on the right-of-way again. It seems as though we can never get more than two days at a time to work on the right-of-way. Charley used his tractor to pull out large logs from the right-of-way. His newly acquired tractor made a huge difference in the amount of work we could accomplish in a day.

We bought a used ATV in March. We believe that we can get into tighter spots in the woods with the ATV than in the truck or even the tractor. We had to take it to the shop for repairs in April and got it back in mid-May. Isn't that the way it goes? You get a piece of equipment to help with the big jobs only to have the machine break down and have to be repaired. That was another expense that was not expected.

It's Thursday, May 18. Well, we have "cut through" on the right-of-way and cleared a path to each approximate pole location so that we could get the tractor in to dig the holes. It also allowed us to precisely locate the "field spot" of each pole's location so the line will be straight except for one angle pole. Papaw had some loggers to cut logs off his property so we talked with them, and they have agreed to finish cutting the big trees for us that are on the right-of-way. They have already cleared out some of the brush and the areas where they cleaned out look much better.

On May 30, Charley cut the trees, and the loggers pulled out the logs. They cleared a big pile of logs in the back of the cabin, and that created a larger space near the cabin. The help of the loggers kept Charley and me from having to do so much of the clearing of the right-of-way, which allowed us to work on other projects and saved our backs, too.

We partially dug three of the holes for the utility poles. We borrowed an auger from Jerry, which will make the job easier. The auger will save Charley a lot of back-breaking work. The holes have been dug about three feet and need to be two and half to three feet deeper. Charley came up with a plan to get an extension made for the auger that would help him to dig the holes deeper to about four-and-a-half feet, if we do not hit rock. Of course, that will still leave one-and-a-half feet that will have to be dug by hand…with lo-o-ong handled post-hole   diggers…the utility type.

Charley digging a hole using the tractor and Jerry's auger.

Wednesday, June 21, the loggers have not worked for nearly three weeks on the right-of-way. One of them has had a kidney stone and has been unable to work, plus with three inches of rain they could not get in to finish clearing. We have needed the rain as we have had only one-tenth of an inch of rain since early May, so we have tried not to get too upset over the lack of work.

Monday, August 7, 2000. We got up at 6 a.m. and went to the right-of-way where we re-staked where some of the utility poles will go. We drove the tractor and equipment from Papaw's house back to the cabin. It was too hot to work as the temperature was 96° when we left the cabin at 12:40 p.m., so we headed to the trailer...very hot and humid. We were exhausted from the heat. All we could think of was a long, cool bath.

On Tuesday, we started drilling on one of the holes for the utility poles. We had to get water to pour in the hole because the ground was so dry that it was too hard to dig the hole. Then it started lightning and thundering, so we went to the cabin and ate lunch. After lunch we went back to the hole. When we stepped out of the truck, we could hear the rain coming up the hollow. It really poured! We decided to call it quits for the day and go home. We were home by two o'clock. We really did not get a lot done today because it was too hot and stormy. The high was 100° with a heat index of 105°.

On Wednesday, Charley finished digging the hole that we started yesterday. It took him a while to finish, and then he was too exhausted to dig anymore for the day. This type of work is exhausting enough on a cool day, but the heat drastically cuts the amount of work that can be done.

We put the generator on the truck so Charley could drill holes in the utility poles to put in spikes for climbing. Papaw came up about 12:30 to help us "set" the first pole. Charley had designed a 20-foot, 2-inch steel pole with a slight bend and a 3-point hitch with a 2000-pound hand winch, so he could use the tractor to set the poles. We worked until about five o'clock, but the boom was not able to lift the pole. We even took the lift boom to Papaw's so he could weld braces on the boom to prevent it from bending, but it did not work.

Charley and I continued working until about six o'clock but we still could not get the winch to raise the pole up. In fact, as we continued to crank the winch, the boom just folded further downward with each crank of the winch. A lot of work went into the design of the boom lift so we left feeling worn out and defeated. (A note from Charley: *A note of defense for the lift pole: We had ordered our power poles from neighboring Lawrenceburg Power System and had specified a class 6 pole which would have been about 1200 pounds, but like most dependable utilities, they had stopped using the smaller class 6 and only used a class 3 or 4 pole for stronger, more durable power lines. This more than doubled the weight of the poles...so thus the folding boom and struggling 2000-pound winch.)*

We went back to Papaw's and while I cooked supper, Papaw and Charley sat at the dining table discussing how to get the poles up without using a boom to lift them.

The gin pole with the utility pole ready to be raised.

Papaw took a napkin that was laying on the table and began to draw. (Papaw worked construc-tion with TVA [Tennessee Val-ley Authority] and local chemical plants of middle Tennessee) and he was very knowledgeable in his field.

Papaw suggested using a "gin pole." Charley and I had never heard of a gin pole. Papaw explained that we could cut a 20 to 25 foot hickory tree, remove all the limbs and snags, and we then could use the gin pole as the stabilizing factor. What does that mean? Well, you put up the gin pole at the edge of the hole that has been dug for the power pole and tie it off in eight to ten direc-tions to stabilize the gin pole. A pulley is attached to an eye bolt at the top and bottom of the gin pole. A cable is run through the top pulley to the pivot point of the utility pole below. The other end of the cable is run from the top pulley through the bottom pulley and attached to the tractor. The tractor is then used to pull away from the gin pole which allows the utility pole to slowly lift upward. When the pole is lifted high enough by the tractor, Charley will swing the butt of the utility pole around so that it will be above the hole where it is to go. The utility pole is then lowered to the bottom of the hole. Now I know your next question: If Charley is at the pole so that he can swing the butt of the pole over the hole, who is driving the tractor?

Well, that would be me...*The Blonde Groundman.* I often wondered if it was safe to let a blonde groundman drive the tractor. A time or two Charley wondered the same thing when I would forget to switch gears, or would lower the pole instead of raising it. Now let's see...do I put it in reverse or first gear? Am I supposed to push in the clutch or let it out? Do I raise the pole or lower the pole? There was so much to think about at one time...with Charley's life resting on my accuracy – and mercy...No, not the time for revenge!

On Tuesday, August 15, we got our first pole up! Hallelujah! Papaw's gin pole really worked! It was 97° when we left there at 3:30 p.m. We all got too hot, but the temperature was not our focus. We really wanted to get one pole done. We were so excited to see that we can set our own poles. Only seven more to go!

On Friday we got another hole almost dug out. We lack about 6 inches, but the hole has rock (this was the sixth hole that we started today) and Charley chipped on it until he could not do anymore. It will be Monday before we will have a chance to get back to work on the hole. Hopefully we will get finished on Monday and we can set that pole on Tuesday. We worked until four o'clock.

Tuesday, August 22, Charley finished digging the second hole today. He got the utility pole and the gin pole to the pole site, and tomorrow he will put the spikes and other hardware on the utility pole. We will set it on Thursday.

Wednesday we got the holes drilled for the spikes* on the utility pole and we got the gin pole set up. Then we had to leave so we could be home for the repair man to fix our air conditioner at the trailer.

*What is the deal of drilling holes for spikes...well, as prior information has revealed, Charley is an engineer/manager by trade and calling...not a lineman. Even though he envied his linemen and their abilities to "float" up and down the poles with ease, he learned by experience that the "Lineman's Calling" was a gift – and art – and not a haphazard hobby.

His experience with climbing included a time when he borrowed a former lineman's hooks and belt when he was at Pulaski (TN) Electric System where he attempted to ascend a pole in his back yard with his four-year old son, Greg...and God...as his only witnesses. About ten minutes into the climb and twenty feet above ground, Greg, in his child-like wisdom said, "Daddy, I think you better come down."

Charley, who recognized a Divine intervention in his son's words, slowly descended (recalling the horror stories of his "old-timer" linemen of their "cut-outs"), and he finally reached the ground some fifteen minutes later.

For this venture of setting our own poles, Charley borrowed Greg's deer-hunting tree-climbing hooks as we started our own power line. Several attempts and twisted ankles later, Charley derived a master plan: a portable fourteen-foot aluminum extension ladder (for intruder safety), followed by deer stand spikes from that point to the top of the pole. Where there's a will...there's a way.

Charley climbing the pole using an aluminum extension ladder and deer stand spikes.

Thursday, we tried to set a pole, but the cable on the come-along broke twice. We then used pulleys and cables and tried to raise it with the 4-wheeler, but it would not work. Then we tried raising it with Papaw's four-wheel-drive truck but the small pulley broke. We went to TSC and got a larger pulley. Before we left the pole site, Charley sprayed diazinon over the area, so hopefully we will not have the no-see-ums and ticks everywhere as we work tomorrow. It felt as though we were being eaten alive by all those insects and Charley and I could not take it any longer.

On Friday, August 25, we set our second pole today! We had the pole in the hole before ten o'clock, but we forgot to "cant" the pole (turning the insulators to the proper alignment), and it took us two-and-a-half hours to correct it. We used the larger pulley and hooked the cable to the truck and raised the pole. It took a while to get everything done. Papaw did not help us on this day as he did not feel well. (This was the only pole that Papaw did not oversee its setting, and we really missed him and his expertise. Maybe that's why we forgot to cant the pole!)

Charley was a little upset because Papaw wanted him to rent a digger derrick to set the remaining poles or hire someone to set the poles for us. Charley called about four places before he found someone who could set the poles, but we had to dig our own holes. They would then charge $75 an hour for travel time, "stuck" time, and time required to set the pole. Charley also knew from his utility experience that most of the pole locations for our poles were not accessible to a digger derrick. Charley decided that we would continue on our own. So we did!

On Tuesday, August 29, well, Charley tried digging the hole at the cabin, but the tractor would not run for long periods at a time. He got it dug about two to three feet, then he had to manually dig with a posthole digger.

Of course, he hit rock. He talked to Jerry who gave him some hints on what to do for the tractor. (More delays as we are continually working on the tractor.)

On Wednesday, September 6, we tried to dig another hole. Well, the auger quit working. It is so frustrating to get one thing working, and then something else break down. I know I should remain positive, but I just get so disheartened over <u>nothing</u> working right. It seems as though we have come to a standstill. Tomorrow has to be better. My head and chest have been hurting today and I feel "listless." Oh well, tomorrow is another day. Temperature was 83° with a light wind... perfect for working...but no equipment with which to work.

On Thursday, we got the hole dug and the gin pole and the utility pole moved to the site. We set the gin pole, and when we tried to straighten the pole with only two ropes attached, it fell!! We got it set up again after one-and-a-half hours. When we tried to tighten the four ropes, the gin pole fell again! I tried to talk Charley into quitting for the day, but he refused to give up. He wanted to try setting up the gin pole one more time.

Charley got the pole up, and when he started tying off the four re-arranged ropes of the gin pole, well...you guessed it...the pole fell for the third time! I burst out laughing! I could not help it! My nerves were shot! The look – no words – that he gave me let me know very quickly that it was not funny. In fact, I believe that if I had been closer to him that he probably would have tied me to that pole...and tried a fourth time!

He was very upset about the gin pole falling for the third time, but I finally convinced him to stop for the day and get a fresh start tomorrow. It was 5:30 p.m. *(I learned one thing today...a groundman does NOT laugh at his [or her] lineman...blonde or not!)*

Although Charley had been in the utility business for over 30 years, he learned something today about setting a gin pole – this completely old concept of utility operation that disappeared with the era of digger derricks and bucket trucks years prior to Charley's utility expertise. So this "old" concept of gin poles was a "new" invention on this power line that was strictly off the beaten path of civilization. His lesson learned today: When setting a gin pole, tie <u>all</u> anchor ropes snugly as you get the gin pole pretty well to a vertical position, to prevent the gin pole from rotating from its present vertical position to a perfect horizontal position...in one second or less. It took three lessons...but he learned this concept well. As with all lineman work: Shortcuts can be <u>very</u> costly – do it right...the first time!

On Friday we got the third pole set (The pole at the end of the bottom). Thank you Lord that everything went so well today. Papaw came to the site and helped us. Once everything was in place it went rather quickly. It was a relief to get the pole set after all that happened yesterday. Charley could not have taken another day like that! The burst of laughter today was a joyous one as we had another pole set. Only five more to go!

On Wednesday, September 13, we got a hole dug to nearly five feet deep. We kept hitting rock, but Charley kept chipping away at the rocks until he could get the hole deeper. It took about three hours to get it dug out. I helped by either holding the steel rod while Charley hammered with a small sledgehammer, or he held the rod while I hammered…a dangerous job to hold while a blonde groundman uses a hammer. My short arms could hardly swing that small sledgehammer over my head (a muscle-building event). But I kept at it because I knew that every swing that I took, prevented Charley from having to swing that sledgehammer, thereby saving his arms and back. It was very tiring, but at least we had results from all our efforts.

While Charley drilled the spike holes in the fourth pole, I sat on the tailgate of the truck and was struck by the beauty of the moment. The trees were green, the sky was vividly blue, and even the curvature of the driveway was perfect. Everything blended together. I felt so at peace as it appeared that the earth was so serene. The birds were singing, a cool breeze was blowing, and the smell of "fresh" was everywhere. It was a good moment. I wish I could experience these moments more often, but there is never enough time for slow moments and just sitting and absorbing God's great creation…and, NO, I did not finally flip out…it was DIVINE – a "God Moment!"

On Friday, we got our fourth pole set. (The one beside our meter pole and nearest to Papaw.) Thank you, Lord. The process went smoothly considering all the work that had to be done to get the hole deep enough to set the pole. Charley was very pleased with the process. Only four more to go...we are halfway through!

Charley and Papaw getting a pole ready to put in place.

On Wednesday, September 27, Charley dug on another hole at the cabin (for the fifth pole). We have it down to nearly four feet deep. As usual, we have hit rock. We have gone through about two feet of rock. It was a very slow and tiring process, especially as we had to swing that sledgehammer one lick at a time.

On Thursday we did get our fifth hole to the needed depth, and the entire pole setting process went without a hitch! Only three more to go! Papaw helped us today. He saw a copperhead snake that was about four feet long. It ran under a brush pile, so when we finished setting the pole, he suggested that we burn the brush pile and run the snake out and kill it. So, we burned the brush pile, but the snake never came out. It either went into a hole, burned up, or it moved on to another location. I really hope it burned up, because I do not like to think about a snake running around loose, particularly at the cabin!

On Tuesday we went back to the hole that we had started near Second Creek. The hole had 18 to 20 inches of water. We tried digging another hole (five times) but kept hitting rock. We finally gave up and went back to the original hole. Charley made a scoop out of tin, and we dipped the water out of the hole. He finally said we would just put the pole in and pile dirt up around it in a large mound to get the hole up to five feet (it was less than five feet deep). So this will be our sixth hole. We will then be three-fourths of the way through with only two more to go.

We used the four-wheeler today. I drove back and forth to the cabin several times to get tools that we needed. I always enjoyed driving the 4-wheeler, as it was a chance to have some fun while we worked.

It is Wednesday, and we are so tired that we can hardly stand. The gin pole is in place. Tomorrow we will put in the sixth pole! We may have to dip the water out of the hole before we can lower the pole. Papaw suggested that we put concrete in the hole after we put in the pole. Charley agreed with Papaw, so that is what we decided to do. We went to Lawrenceburg to get the concrete before we went to church.

This hole was requiring a lot more work and I prayed that this would not be the pattern for the next two poles. Charley and I would like to see the next two poles up before his interview for general manager with an area utility on October 18 (See Chapter 8).

I don't know how Charley holds up to do so much. He works tirelessly all day, every day, doing such strenuous work. Today's temperature was in the upper 80s to low 90s. It was very hot, but there was a little shade where we were working.

On Thursday we put up our sixth pole near "Second Creek." Only two more to go! Thank you, Lord. It was a lot of work. We had to dip the water out of the hole. Papaw was late getting to the site, so Charley and I set the pole ourselves. Papaw got there just as we got it set. We mixed up four bags of concrete and poured it in the hole.

Then we had to haul dirt to finish filling the hole and mound up around the pole. Papaw suggested that we use his small trailer, so we went to get it from his barn. When we found the trailer we realized that it had a tire that was coming apart so Charley and I took the tire and wheel to Turnpike Tire Center to get another tire and tube for the trailer. It cost us $12 and a couple of hours. Just one more piece of equipment that had to be worked on! We took the trailer to use it, but we could never get the tractor scoop high enough to dump the dirt onto the trailer.

So, we had to unhitch the trailer and hook up our big trailer. With our trailer Charley could back the tractor onto the trailer and then dump the dirt. It took us about twenty minutes to put the dirt on the trailer. Then we used shovels to unload the dirt and spread it around the pole. It took us an hour-and-a-half to do this job. We may have to add more dirt later, but with the concrete and dirt, we were at proper depth. We were at the cabin by eight o'clock that morning, and we left around seven o'clock that evening. It was a very, very long day.

On Tuesday, October 10, we put both the gin pole and the utility pole on our 16 foot trailer. It took us over three hours to get them moved from the cabin to the angle pole site near Papaw's. It was stressful. The truck could not pull the trailer over a long hill of our driveway, so we had to take the tractor and pull the truck and trailer over the hill. I drove the tractor and Charley drove the truck except when we pulled the truck over the hill. All of it was stressful worrying whether or not we could get the poles to the site safely.

We moved everything up to the angle pole. We then had to clear out some of the brush and logs that were left by us and the loggers. (A note from Charley: *Surprisingly, the 2800-plus feet of power line ended up with only one real angle, plus another less-than-one-degree angle [which was keyed, or braced, with a rock to offset that small angle]. This virtually straight line was laid out on a USGS map through wooded area with a creek and small branch [stream] as guide points for the original engineering of the entire line. But, to our surprise, the final line survey came out perfectly with the projected USGS layout...with a lot of prayer).*

Thursday, October 12, Charley got the hole deep enough (about five-and-a-half feet) so that we can set the angle pole. This will be the seventh hole dug. Only one more to go and it will be a doozy. Solid Rock! Anyway, we are going to try to set the gin pole in the morning and perhaps the utility pole tomorrow afternoon. Charley says we just have to see how it goes. He tries not to get too enthusiastic because he knows what obstacles we are up against.

Friday, October 13th: We got the gin pole set up today. It was very trying. It took us all day! It took a while to get the pole up because the hillside was so uneven that it was difficult to get the tractor right where we needed it. When Charley tried to move the utility pole over to the hole, the tractor reared up twice. I was so afraid that it was going to flip over. Charley was very concerned *(afraid)*, too.

Before we could get the pole moved, the tractor quit and we could not get it going again. We finally decided that it was not meant for us to set the pole today, so we quit for the day. It was already after four o'clock. Did you notice the date? Friday the 13th!! And we are not even superstitious!

Monday, October 16, well, we got the tractor running, again. We had tried everything we knew to do. Charley even went to Papaw's and got his tractor to try to pull off our tractor and then use Papaw's tractor to set the pole. Papaw's tractor could not get enough traction to pull our tractor, so we were right back where we started.

Papaw walked up to where we were and he and Charley looked at the tractor to try and determine the problem. They decided to take off the carburetor and look at it. Then they took the carburetor to Papaw's house and saw that there was a rubber tipped part that was stuck. While they worked on the carburetor, I cleaned the kitchen, washed a load of clothes, and cooked lunch for all of us.

Charley put the carburetor back on the tractor, and it started without any problems. He then came back to Papaw's and we ate lunch. After lunch we went back to the pole site to set the pole. It was about four o'clock when we had everything ready to go.

Charley went to get Papaw and saw his (Papaw's) neighbor, W. H., who was in his yard. Charley told him that we were getting ready to set the pole, so he and Jeanne came to watch us.

Using Charley's tractor, the pole went up fairly easy. Then when we lowered it into the hole, the pole hung at about four-and-a-half feet. We pushed it, pulled it, even tried to lift it back out of the hole, but all to no avail. The pole would not budge. Nothing worked. Charley tried to lift it out of the hole by using the tractor, but the roller that was used with the pulley at the bottom of the gin pole snapped and flew off. (It is amazing Charley was not hit by that flying roller!!) Papaw suggested that we pour water into the hole to see if the pole would slide on down. But that did not work. Charley and Papaw decided that maybe when it rained that, just maybe, the pole might slide on down into the hole, eventually. Anyway, that is our prayer. Being the angle pole, it cannot go any direction but down to the bottom of the hole. (*Charley checked the pole the next day and it had lowered within a few inches of the bottom of the hole. We did not make the October 18 deadline, but we were close. But Charley did go for his GM interview – detailed in Chapter 8).*

On Friday, October 20, Charley and I loaded all the tools on the truck to prepare for the eighth pole. He took everything to the hole and unloaded the truck while I went to Papaw's to cook lunch for all of us.

Charley did have one more close encounter while I was preparing lunch. As he started off the hillside on the tractor toward the proposed pole site, he was in second gear, and the tractor was idled a little high as he started down-hill. He finally realized he needed to slow down a bit, so he clutched to shift to first gear. Well, he learned one thing about his new tractor: It has a double clutch and going down-hill is not the time to push the clutch.

*Papaw, Charley and me pulling the ropes to
the utility pole in preparation for pole setting.*

To summarize...that tractor took off like a bat out of...well let's just say it was headed for the bluff's edge at a high rate of speed...a 50-foot drop into good ol' Brush Creek. But with some Divine planning – unbeknown to us – and with Divine wisdom at the instant that Charley cried for help, he quickly turned the tractor into a brush pile that we had stacked just to the left of his path downward to the creek.

Just another day in the life of our adventurous journey! Oh, did I forget to mention that Charley did pause to offer a word of "Thanks" to his Intercessor, before he backed the tractor from his refuge of brush?

Charley tried using the star drill to chip out the rock of this final hole, but it did not work too well.

So, he tried another hole that we had started. He got that one down to about four feet and said "that's enough" so, we are ready to set the last pole!!

Charley checking the line to see if it has proper sag.

Charley remembered from his utility days that we can put a framework around this pole to a height of two feet and add rebar and concrete in the form to get our six feet of depth in-ground.

Tuesday, October 24, 2000. Thank you, Lord!! The eighth and last pole went up today!! We still need to fill in the hole and pour the concrete in the hole around the pole since we could only get it down four feet. (Charley and Papaw both think that it would be best if we pour concrete around the pole.)

And, of course, there was a hitch along the way. Charley had used the tractor to lift the pole so the butt would clear the hole and it would be ready to set in the hole. Then Charley had me to get on the tractor so that I could lower the pole as he guided the pole into the hole. The tractor was idling and when I got on the tractor I put it in first gear, which made the pole lift instead of lower.

Charley began to yell, "Take it out of gear! Take it out of gear and use the brake" to ease the tractor back down the hillside. The hillside was very steep and I was afraid that I would roll off the hill, but I managed to ease it down the way he needed me to so that the pole could go to the bottom of the hole. After the pole reached the bottom of the hole, I eased the tractor back a little further so that he would have the slack he needed to remove the cable from the tractor.

This picture of me on the tractor was taken from the video that W. H. made for us. I had to stand up to get enough pressure on the brake.

W. H. and Jeanne Bancroft came up to the pole site while we were putting up the pole. They videotaped us working and setting the pole. (*Later it was great getting to watch the video. It was amazing to see – live – what we had been doing.*) As we were always working, we did not have many pictures of us actually doing the work. Even a *blonde groundman* can reason out that you cannot take pictures of yourself doing work. Smarter than you thought, right? Well, I did reason out that this video of this last pole could verify that I was there, and actually working...driving the tractor.)

On Thursday we got the concrete poured in the last hole today. We went to Lawrenceburg to get the concrete mix and some lumber to build the frame around the pole. We also did our early voting for the Presidential election. We went to the cabin and got the tools needed to work at the pole, and then went to Papaw's to cut the boards for the frame. While Charley cut the boards, I went in at Papaw's and folded clothes, made his bed, and cooked lunch for all of us.

After lunch, Charley and I went up to the last pole to do the work that needed to be done there. We had to let the gin pole down and tie off the utility pole. We used fourteen bags of concrete mix to fill up the hole. We used a 55-gallon drum of water to feed through a garden hose with a faucet attached to the end of the hose so that we could turn the water on and off as needed. What a great idea. Charley and Papaw both thought of that. We worked until nearly six o'clock, and then we gathered up all the tools and Papaw's stuff and took them back to his barn. We are very tired after the full day.

Wednesday, November 15, we pulled the first conductor through for the first three poles. Charley pulled the wire by hand with me rolling the reel (that was in the back of the truck at the meter pole near Papaw's house) so the wire would be easier for him to pull. After that,

Charley used the 4-wheeler. What a difference that 4-wheeler made. He could pull the wire so much faster and not have to do nearly as much walking.

Jerry had suggested that we use walkie-talkies (which he had and allowed us to borrow). This helped us to communicate with each other. Charley would let me know when he was stopping so I could put the brake on to stop the wire. Then he would let me know when he was starting up again so I could take the brake off. (We had to keep the communication simple, because Charley could not understand well over the walkie-talkies with his hearing problem.)

Did I mention that Charley had built a reel rack with a stop brake for controlling the output of the #4 ACSR conductors that was on a wooden reel? At each pole Charley had the pull-lines run through a small pulley on top of the pole – one for the hot conductor and one for the neutral conductor - just as his linemen had always done. Who says management cannot learn from linemen? Charley would pull his rope that was tied to the conductor through the pulley first and then use the rope to pull the conductor through the pulley at each pole.

After we finished pulling the first conductor, Charley and I went to the cabin and put up a few things and looked at the area of the ceiling that he had started. It was beginning to look more like a livable cabin. It will be a slow process, but I think it will look great when it is finished.

On Monday, November 27, we pulled the second wire. Charley is tired from all the walking and pulling wire. He pulled his back and had a lot of pain. My hips were sore from where I stood in an awkward positon at the reel brake in the back of the pickup. Our bodies are wearing out from all of the wear and tear.

On Tuesday, Charley went to the cabin and put in an anchor for the guy wire and installed the other hardware on the pole. On Wednesday he worked at several poles where he put hardware on the poles, and lifted the conductor to the top insulator of the pole. He then loosely tied a tie wrap so the conductor could slip for proper sagging. He climbed several of the poles four and five times each, and he was worn out from all of the climbing.

On Friday, December 1, 2000, Charley worked on lifting the line conductor up to the top of several more poles. The generator did not work properly so he went to Waynesboro to get a new filter for the generator.

After lunch he helped Papaw finish installing the wench no his (Papaw's) truck. Papaw wanted the wench so that he would not have to lift the deer into the truck when he killed one. Later, Charley worked in the cabin putting up cover plates on outlets and light switches. He had a full day of work.

Wednesday, January 3, 2001, we went to Russellville, Kentucky to get some spare transformers. We bought them from Russellville Electric System. They loaded five transformers in the bed of our little red

Sonoma pick up. They would have put more on the truck, but five was all it would hold. We paid $100 for the five "junk-but-good" transformers. These transformers will be used for backup in case we have one of our existing two transformers to short out.

Driving home was a real experience as the front of the truck "floated" along the highway, because the bed of the truck was so heavy with the transformers. We could not get up a lot of speed due to the "floating" which made our trip take longer than we expected. We prayed continuously that Charley would be able to hold the truck in the road and we would get home safely. Even though we were excited to get the transformers, it was stressful bringing them home. Someday we will get a heavy-duty truck so that we can haul equipment more safely!

On Saturday, Charley and I took the transformers down to the cabin. Greg was there hunting, and he came over and helped us. We sure were glad to see him. Charley had to use a hoist to get the transformers out of the truck and Greg was able to help him do the heavy lifting.

Tuesday, January 16, we tried to install the hardware on the remaining poles, but it was so cold that we could hardly work. The pole was so hard the bit could hardly penetrate the wood. Charley got one of the holes drilled in the angle pole. (That is the pole that stuck before hitting the bottom of the hole.) So since we could not cant the pole, we had to re-drill for proper alignment for its hardware. Charley got a headache from the cold, and everything seemed to be going wrong, so we left. Some days were so frustrating that we felt as though we would have accomplished more if we had stayed in bed…and probably would have been a lot more fun!

It's Wednesday, February 7 and we worked on the poles today. Charley got all the holes drilled in the poles. With all the climbing, drilling, and ladder set-ups, the work day was full.

On Thursday we went to the Lawrenceburg Power System to get some things needed to finish our power line. It was all old, used scrap material and reasonably priced, but it was very useful for this back-woods power line.

Tuesday, February 20, well, today was cloudy and windy with a temperature in the mid-60s. We finished the pole at the cabin except for the underground wire to the cabin. We got the guy wires re-pulled at the corner pole where they had gotten knocked down when we cut a tree.

We also worked at the pole next to the meter pole near Papaw's. We got the guywire on it, and now we are ready to pull the lines to the proper tightness (pull out the slack) that they need to be – or, to the linemen, we are ready to *sag* the line! All of this is slow work, but we are much closer to getting our electricity.

Wednesday, February 21, what a day! Charley rode the line to make sure the poles and line are okay to pull. They are. He found several trees that needed to be cut, so we borrowed Papaw's chainsaw and began to cut.

We had a time of it. The chain came off so I had to go to Papaw's and get a screw driver and a crescent wrench. Then we had to tie off the tree so it would fall away from the line. I pulled the long rope and hid behind a large tree. A small tree-top branch hit me on the top of the head, but luckily I had on a toboggan and a hooded jacket which padded my head (and, of course, my head is the hardest part about me...underneath that blonde decor).

On another tree cut, I cranked the come-along and cranked it too tight, and the cable got hung in the spool. Charley had to work about thirty minutes to get it fixed. Even though he was very frustrated, he did not yell at me although he could have justifiably done so. He said it could have happened to him. It took us 30 to 45 minutes to cut down a huge beech tree. It was a beautiful tree, but it was too close to the line...it had to go.

Charley told me to go across the fence to the sand bar at Second Creek so that I would be well away from the large tree that he was cutting down. He seemed to take forever to cut the tree so I began to wander around, looking at the pretty rocks in the creek.

I looked beyond the fence and realized that our tools were in the path where that tree would fall, so I went across the fence to move our tools. About the time that I crawled over the fence, Charley had sawed through the tree, and I heard a 'craaack' as the tree was ready to fall.

Charley looked to make sure that I was still out of harm's way, and when he saw that I was standing in the path of the tree he began to yell, "Run! The tree is falling! RUN NOW!!" I took off running and cleared the fence just as the tree fell...tools in hand! It barely missed me.

Of course, Charley gave me a good talking too. I know...he should have yelled at me for moving and not staying where I was. Well, at least the tools were moved before the tree landed. I mean, we could have had to dig those tools out from under all those branches on that huge tree. Personally, I feel as though I did a good deed...not so smart, but good!

It appears that I have a guardian angel watching out for me. With two mishaps in one day...both of which I could have been killed or seriously injured, I walked away without a scratch...with the Good Lord's help. A blonde groundman can be dangerous! *Shock Therapy* is the right term!

Charley and I are very sore tonight from all the work. Well, Charley worked and I ran for my life!

On Thursday we got the slack out of the lines and sagged them, so the top and neutral lines were equal distance apart throughout the full distance of the power line. It was tedious work. We had to walk the line several times to be sure the lines were sagged properly. Charley walked it more than I did. I was impressed at how much he had learned from his linemen over the years. They did a good job on him.

The pole at the cabin started leaning slightly, and when Charley tried pulling the guywire, a clamp gave way. We had to go to the opposite end of the line, let off on the lines that we still had tied off, and re-pull and re-clamp the guywire at the cabin. We had to go back and forth several times, but we got it done.

Charley mounting fuse cut-out above the transformer.

On Friday we got the second and last trans-former up at the MLEC meter pole. Everything is looking good. While Charley made all the connections to the trans-former, I went to Papaw's and put his clean sheets on his bed, folded clothes, washed dishes, swept the dining room and kitchen, and warmed him some lunch. I then went back to the pole where Charley and I ate our lunch.

We had peanut butter and crackers and cookies. I tried to take care of Papaw...Charley and I ate whatever was the easiest and quickest when we were in the field working the power line. A big meal and heavy work do not always go together. Charley was all over that pole to-day, and I know he is exhausted. We are still hoping to be in our cabin by the first of April.

Monday, February 26, we cleaned at the cabin and stored away the tools that we used to put up the poles, wire, transformers and other surplus hardware for the poles. We stored things outside that were weatherproof to give us more room inside. It took all day, but at least we have things put away.

Tuesday morning we went to Hohenwald to meet with the electrical inspector. He told us some things that we needed to re-do. We were discouraged because it will set us back some, but we will get it done.

*Charley putting up the last trans-
former at the meter pole.*

We went back to the cabin and Charley "finished out" the towel closet, closet doors, utility room door and the garage door. I finished chipping the concrete, and then washed down and painted the bathroom floor.

After we left the cabin, we went home, let Sully out to do business, and then went to Lowe's in Columbia to get the conduit and wire (that we could not get in Florence). Of course, while we were out and about we had to eat a good meal, so we ate at the Golden Corral. Lowe's had the wire but not the conduit.

Wednesday we went back to Hohenwald to get conduit because Lowe's in Columbia did not have it in stock. We got a late start because we needed to make some phone calls and do other things at the trailer.

When we went to the cabin, Charley planted some trees that we received from the Arbor Day Foundation, and I cleaned out some of the stuff in the cabin side, in preparation for the carpet. After we got back to the trailer, Charley went to Lawrenceburg to get some more materials that he needed at the cabin. He then studied for his Wednesday night class for church.

Thursday, March 1, we were in Lawrenceburg by 7:30 a.m. to get a ditch witch to dig trenches for the electrical and water lines. It was a nightmare to use. Charley had a terrible time maneuvering the ditch witch, because it was so heavy, and the ground was so rough. It was a hand-operated machine versus the riding type, so it really worked Charley over good. It was amazing how much he was able to get done with it.

He cut our telephone line, and now he has to fix that. We had to have the ditch witch back by noon, so it pushed us to get it back in time, but we made it before the deadline.

We then went back to the cabin and cleaned out the trench for the electrical line. We are very exhausted tonight, especially Charley. I am afraid that he will be sore tomorrow from all the "bronco riding" with the ditch witch, and then cleaning out the trench.

The weather this week has been perfect with temperatures in the mid-to-low 60s and plenty of sunshine. We are getting closer to moving. Lord, please let us be able to move by April 1 (even if it is April Fool's Day)!

Friday, we cleaned out the trench at the meter pole. It was very slow going because there were so many roots and rocks. At noon I walked down the hill to Papaw's and warmed up spaghetti and made cornbread for lunch. I also made his bed and folded his clothes.

Charley is very sore due to operating the ditch witch *(with this hand-held ditch witch, he had to control it with his upper body...and with all the work he has been doing, he does not have much upper body left.)* I am not as sore as I have been. My back actually feels better than it has in two weeks. Both of us have been wearing back braces and those seem to help. Today we wore knee pads, and they were very helpful as we were on our knees a lot cleaning out the trenches. It began to rain about 2:30 or so, and by 4:00 we had to quit because it was raining too hard for us to work.

On Tuesday, March 6, Charley and I worked at the cabin during the morning. We finished the trim work, painting and staining. In the afternoon Charley worked at the meter pole and I continued working at the cabin. We are so very close to being finished…if only we can get our electricity and water finished. And if we could only work more than one day at a time.

On Wednesday, March 14, Charley and I went to six of the poles to finish tying off the conductors to the insulators. Our time ran out on us so we had to quit before we could get through. The inspector is supposed to come tomorrow. Please, Lord, let the inspection pass and let us get our electricity!

It's Thursday, March 15, and our inspection passed!! Thank you, Lord! Hallelujah!! We are so very excited. The inspector was very impressed that Charley and I did the power line ourselves. In fact, when Charley first told him about our project and the work we had done I believe that he was a little skeptical. As he and Charley talked, he began to realize that we could not have made up some of the stories that Charley shared with him.

After the inspection I drove to Hohenwald to the Meriwether Lewis Electric Cooperative (MLEC) to pay for the inspection. MLEC installed the meter and has us hooked up and ready to go after a few finishing touches on our poles.

We can hardly believe it...we have electricity! As with any good electrical system, we do have "safety first" on our power line. We have a 200 Amp breaker at the meter pole and a 2400 volt fuse cut-out on the high side of the transformer pole for "air safety" when doing any work on "our" power line.

As groundman, Kathy was able to pitch the smaller tools to Charley's hands above, with almost perfect placement (after much practice).

Of course, the story of the power line does not end here. There is continual maintenance as we have to keep the right-of-way cleared (we have had a bull dozer in a couple of times to clear out the underbrush and stumps). We have had one outage on "our" line which occurred about six months after Charley used "Spike" to kill the stump growth under the line. The slight slope of the hillside let the "Spike" effects reach the lower saplings beyond our right-of-way. A 50-foot sapling died and fell mid-span of one span of the line, which pushed the hot conductor into the neutral and kicked the 200 Amp breaker at the meter pole. We opened the line, cut the tree, and were back in business in less than an hour. Considering the storms and lightning that continually hit the area, we have certainly been blessed!

Charley and Paul, his brother, try to bush hog the right-of-way as often as they can, but it grows fast, and we continue to walk the line to make sure there are no problems. Greg, our son, will use his 4-wheeler to ride the line when he is at the cabin for his hunting weekends. So, the power line lives on...not just in this book but in reality...some 14 years later!

The utility pole at the top of the gin pole ready to be swung over the hole and lowered by the tractor. Notice all the line ropes attached to the top of the gin pole. Can you imagine why that gin pole fell three times?

In our defense of the 18 months of calendar time required for the power line, we actually only had 40 working days per the journal documentation. We feel that compared to the 100 plus years of Noah's project, we did pretty good…and there were days that we felt we needed to switch projects and build an ark, with all of the rain. But as the other chapters reveal, procrastination was not our delay! We <u>were</u> busy!

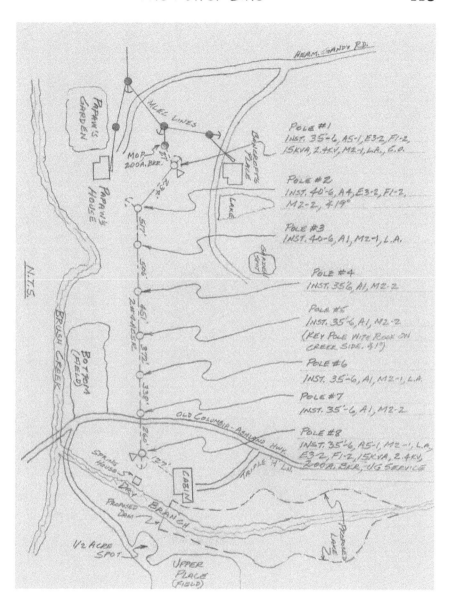

Working Drawing of Power Line Layout

Kathy is yelling to Charley, "If you fall, I will catch you!"

CHAPTER 5
Papaw

During the month of June, 1999, we helped Papaw, Charley's dad (who was 80 years old at the time) with his garden and other farming chores. Most of the garden planting was done in early May, but the tasks to do afterwards were endless. A former steamfitter, job superintendent, and union business agent, Papaw's mind never ceased to derive new projects for each day...and upcoming week, even at his ripe old age. So our days were packed...and our new dream had not even started.

Papaw was working on the upper place (an upper level field on his property about a mile from his house) with bush hogging and disking. His old tractor (1948 Farmall) broke down continuously, and Charley and he would work on it to keep it running.

One day in particular, the tractor broke down on a hill as Papaw was coming out of the bottom (a field near the creek located on our proposed cabin plot). We had gone to Pulaski, Tennessee to deliver our piano to Greg (our son) as he had agreed to keep it for us. (We did not have room for it in the trailer.)

It was a church night (Wednesday) and Papaw had no way of contacting us (he did not use a cellphone and if he had had one, it would not have helped him because there are no cellphone towers close enough to provide coverage), so he had to walk home which was about 2.4 miles total with about half of it uphill. The 2.4 miles was around the roads – actually just over a half-mile down the rough terrain of the creek. After we returned home from church, we called Papaw to check on him, and he told us about the tractor breaking down and him having to walk home. Charley and I went to our cabin site to see if we could get Papaw's tractor going, but we could not get it started. We could not drive past the tractor because it was blocking the narrow and rough roadway out of the field in the bottom. So, Charley pushed in the clutch and let the tractor roll back into some brush and against a log. Charley then thought he would use our pickup to push the front of the tractor around so that we could let the tractor roll on down the hill to a flat place at the bottom.

Our truck (1992 GMC Sonoma) could not even budge that tractor! That little red pick-up spun for all it was worth, but it was no match for that Farmall! Then, to double the jeopardy, the truck was against the tractor and on a slick hill. So the tractor would not budge and the truck could not get enough traction to back up.

It took us a while, and with the help of a few boards, we were finally able to get the truck backed up far enough to get to the bottom to turn around. It was now after nine o'clock. *(Isn't it amazing how time makes these tragic moments seem so amusing now?)*

The next day we were able to get the tractor started (after some tinkering around) and back to Papaw's shop so that he could fix the tractor and finish his bush hogging.

On July 28, 1999, Papaw gathered about a dozen ears of Hickory King corn with the announcement that our first major corn gathering would be Saturday, July 31. He was correct in his predictions and on Saturday, 965 ears of corn were gathered by Papaw, Bud (Charley's cousin), and Charley. Charley's older sisters, Connie and Sandy, and Sandy's husband, Jack, came later to assist with the project.

The men shucked and silked the corn outside, while the ladies cut the corn off the cob and processed the corn for the freezer at the dining room table. It would make for excellent eating throughout the winter. It was a hard day of work, but everyone enjoyed the fellowship of family. The process continued up until mid-August, with the remainder of the work process covered fully by Papaw, Charley and me.

The total amount of corn processed for this year was 1,995 ears. *(In case we forgot to mention, Papaw was a competitive gardener, fisherman, hunter, and everything else he attempted to do. He had a lady friend, Ann, at church that he was always in competition with to see who could get the most corn, beans, potatoes, and any other produce they planted. The competition kept both of them energized, and helped them forget their ages and just trudge on. Even more importantly, Papaw was a tither –*

10% plus – of his time, money, and...yes, garden. The first-fruits – the best – went to the preacher. I guess that's why he was so blessed – and we were so busy – preserving his abundant blessings!)

On Tuesday, August 10, we cooked lunch at Papaw's, went to watch more of the roadwork to our cabin being done, and then returned to Papaw's to clean up the kitchen from lunch. Charley helped Papaw shell peas that Papaw had picked during the morning. After they finished shelling the peas, we prepared them for the freezer. Charley and I went home, cut off the corn from Monday, and prepared it for the freezer. It was another long, hot day with bedtime at 10:30 never feeling so good.

On Friday, August 27, Charley and I spent the day bush hogging. We were at Papaw's by about 9:00 and took the tractor and bush hog to the upper field. The view from the upper place was spectacular! There was nothing around the field except trees and the blue, cloudless sky. It was a beautiful setting...except that Charley found a couple of nests of bumble bees. He decided to avoid those areas with the bush hog. We ate our lunch in the field and concluded our bush hogging about 4:30...with the encouragement of the bumble bees *(Charley has this huge fear of being stung by anything that stings!)*. We went home, took baths, and walked about a mile. It was an enjoyable and beautiful day with comfortable 80s temperature.

Saturday found us again in the field by nine and ready to bush hog. We had parked the tractor on a hill so that we could roll it off and start it, if all else failed...and all else failed! *(Let me insert here that this 1948 Farmall had a back-up plan for starting – a hand crank handily wrapped around the base of the seat – if all else failed. The only problem with cranking the tractor is that in case of over choking, the flooding could create an engine backfire that could turn the cranker a flip...or break an arm – thus the parking on the hill).* When we tried rolling the tractor off, it would not budge. Charley finally saw that the right rear tire was flat.

We went to Papaw's shop to get tools and a jack, and Papaw went back to the upper place with us where we removed the tire. The three of us took it to Lawrenceburg to get it fixed. While we were waiting for the tire to be repaired, we ate lunch at the Country Kitchen (no cooking today!). We picked up the repaired tire, went back to the field, and had the tire back on by 3:30. I took Papaw home and went back up to the field to stay with Charley in case the tractor should quit on him...or the quieted bumble bees should rise again. The tractor quit several times which caused more frustration.

We pulled it off with the truck five or six times to start it. Charley would re-adjust the points each time, but we finally had to give it up about 5:30. We could not get the tractor to run smoothly at all. We tried to drive it back to Papaw's, but the tractor would not run long enough to get it there. We had to leave it in the bottom. Papaw said that we would work on it on Monday. We went home, took our baths, and rested. Temperatures were in the low 90s and very hot and humid...no walking today!

On Monday, August 30, we went to Papaw's, and he and Charley pulled the tractor back to the barn using Papaw's truck. They took off the alternator and the starter. After lunch Papaw took the parts to Lawrence-burg to get them checked and rewired if needed. Since we could not do any work with the tractor, we went home and rested for a while.

Thursday, September 2, found Charley and me at the upper field to finish the bush hogging. We arrived at Papaw's by 9:00 and finished by 5:30. We took about a fifteen minute lunch break. It was a very hot and dry day with the temperature in the mid-90s...but no bumble bees!

On Monday, September 20, Papaw, Charley, and I sowed wheat and clover in the upper place, the half-acre lot (a small plot of ground next to the upper field that was once used as a garden spot by Charley's grandparents), and the bottom. After completing the upper field and half-acre lot, the tractor broke down – again – so we used Papaw's truck to disc and sow fertilizer, and our truck to sow the wheat and clover in the bottom.

Charley had me to drive the truck while he sowed the wheat and clover off the tailgate. When I let off the clutch and pressed the accelerator, the truck jumped forward over a clod of dirt, which caused Charley to nearly fall off the tailgate. When he yelled for me to not press the accelerator so hard, I thought something was wrong so I slammed on the brakes. Well, the sudden stop caused Charley – who was already off balanced from the start – to fall backward into the bed of the truck, where he was covered in flying seed.

Of course, this action did not go without a lecture on how to drive the truck. Well, I have been driving a stick shift since I was about fifteen years old, but driving a graveled roadbed and a lumpy plowed field are two entirely different driving ventures…but I patiently listened to his lecture without comment. *(The deer and turkeys thanked us many times for the extra thick foliage in this spot. Papaw thanked us as well because that spot just happened to be within shooting range of his favorite low-on-the-ground deer stand. He finally submitted to the lower tree stands after he fell 30 feet from a high stand and spent 49 days in intensive care at a local hospital during the 1970s).* We started about 10:00 a.m. with our disking and sowing, and finished up about 6:00. The temperature was in the upper 80s. It rained about one-half inch. Hallelujah! We desperately needed the rain.

On Friday, September 24, Charley and Papaw worked on the tractor (a never-ending job) while I picked two large garbage bags of mustard greens, cleaned the kitchen, and did laundry. We put 16 pints of mustard greens in the freezer.

Monday, September 27, found us at Papaw's where he and Charley cleaned out some of the underbrush along Papaw's road. I picked two large garbage bags of mustard greens and prepped them for the freezer.

Thanksgiving Day was spent at Papaw's. There were 35 to 40 people for lunch. There was so much food that everyone was sufficiently stuffed for the day. It was great to see everyone, and to take a day off from working on the cabin and other projects.

Christmas Eve, 1999. We spent the day baking pies, and smoking a ham and turkey for supper at Papaw's. There were 46 people at his house for supper. *(Forty-six people in a one thousand square foot house called for each person to move only as the one in front of you moved. The men sat at the table, and everyone reached across the men to fill their plates from the bowls on the table. The bedrooms, living room, and back porch were all utilized for eating spots...but no one complained because it was Christmas...and family time. These are some of the most wonderful memories of Christmas in the Gandy family home).* It was a great evening of fellowship and fun. Although Sandy was very sick, she still did the Christmas story – word for word, from memory, as she does every year. Connie led the Christmas songs, and Paul had the prayer of "thanks" for the blessings on each of us. Christmas Eve at Papaw's was always a warm and fuzzy time with family and friends getting together.

There was plenty of food. Connie worked very hard on the food preparations, and others brought dishes to supplement Connie's chicken and dumplings and dressing. She even had a general store for the small children so they could pick out their own toys...and bags of towels and washcloths for the married couples. It was all a neat and cute idea. The children (and adults) loved it! Connie, having never married, adopted everyone as her "children".

Saturday, January 22, 2000, we celebrated Papaw's 81st birthday (whose birthday is actually the 21st). Sandy, Jack, Paul, Trisha, Papaw, Charley and I were together to help him celebrate. The weather was too bad with snow and sleet for Connie and Jen to make the trip from Nashville (Jen was upset that she could not be there and planned to come another day). Papaw was sick with the flu, but he enjoyed everyone being with him and making a fuss over his birthday. And, today, the 22nd is my 49th birthday, so it was a double celebration for the two of us.

Charley and Papaw cutting the tree down in the garden.

Saturday, February 6, Jen had planned to come to Papaw's today because she did not get to come on his birthday due to inclement weather…but today's weather would not allow her to come either. Maybe next week.

On February 9 and 11, we cleaned out blueberry bushes and cut down the big tree from the garden that had died out and was "an accident waiting to happen."

It's Saturday, February 19, and Jen was finally able to come down to spend time with Papaw, Sandy, Charley and me. She brought a pork roast and I cooked some vegetables from the freezer and biscuits and gravy.

After we finished lunch Jen and Sandy began to act suspicious. Jen sent Sandy into the living room while she (Jen) went to the back bedroom. They were giggling like two little school girls. Jen kept saying, "Y'all stay at the table. We'll be right back. Don't move now. Stay there."

Then they would start giggling again. After a few moments of anticipation, Jen walked into the room with a cake with a lit candle, and a song began playing from

the front room: *"Green Acres is the place to be. Farm livin' is the life for me. Land spreadin' out so far and wide. Keep Manhattan, just give me that countryside."*

By then we were rolling in our seats. Jen had gotten a cake with a picture of Eddie Albert and Eva Gabor standing in front of a barn as they did on the "Green Acres" television show. She felt that our wild adventures with our cabin and power line were much like "Green Acres" – especially as there was no cell phone accessibility except at certain high spots (at least we did not have to climb a pole to use the phone at those high spots). This was the third cake that Jen had ordered for my birthday. The first cake she was able to cancel due to the weather, the second cake she was not able to cancel because there was no warning of the weather, so she and Joe (her husband) had to eat that cake. As they say: "third time's a charm," so she was able to come home to Papaw's with the third cake. The whole thing was hilarious. Again, laughter is good for the soul!

Jen also gave me a little clock with a fishing pole as a gift. We had a blast reminiscing about all the effort that she had to put into this surprise. So, as usual, I celebrated my birthday more than one day.

It was February 22, 2000. Time was slipping away. We were well into yet another year. We spent part of our day with Papaw – cooking, cleaning, and helping him with things that he needed to get done.

On Tuesday, May 2, we helped Papaw in his garden during the afternoon. We planted two rows of blue lake green beans; one row each of butterbeans, white field peas, purple hull peas; and ten and a half rows of Hickory King corn. We were all exhausted but glad to get it done.

On Saturday, May 27, we attended the Gandy Family reunion in Russellville, Alabama that is held on "the Saturday before the fourth Sunday" in May of every year. Papaw went with us and he was thrilled to spend time with his cousin, Susie Gandy Vandiver. They had not seen each other in nearly 70 years.

Papaw told us later that she was about sixteen years old the last time he saw her…she was 85 years old at the time of the reunion. Papaw was also glad to meet some of his other relatives for the first time. We also carried a huge crock pot full of venison roast with a nice rich, natural gravy, which was devoured with compliments of being the best "beef roast" that they had ever tasted. After all was eaten and we revealed that it was a deer roast, I think a few almost lost that meal...but I think it was actually from overeating!

Charley and I had planned for this "reunion" day for several weeks. We had decided that we would leave early for the reunion that usually started around two o'clock, and take Papaw to see some of the places where he had lived as a child and during his early adult life. We took our camera for taking pictures and a notebook to keep notes of what Papaw told us about each site. He took us to places where he had lived, churches he had attended, places he had worked, and the baseball field where he played baseball as a teenager. We did not know that he had played baseball as a teenager, and that he was a very good player.

He also told us about some of his "wild oats" teenage years that Charley had never heard of before. Charley was waiting for him to die so he could seek "Sainthood" for him. He backed off of that notion after he realized that his dad was human after all, and had had a normal childhood just like the rest of us. *(Note: We worked on a loose-leaf book of Papaw's memories, added the pictures we took on this day, and gave it to Papaw's five children for Christmas, 2000. More on this project will appear in late December. He and I met several times and went over the notes and pictures to insure that we had recorded the information correctly. After we had everything in book form, he edited and re-edited the book before we printed the final product. The story was printed in first person with Papaw telling the stories of his childhood. His children had not heard many of the stories that were written. When Papaw died in a boating accident in 2004, several of his grandchildren requested copies of his book, as well.)*

On Wednesday, May 31, we helped Papaw in the garden. It was an all-day job but the garden looked great. It was the prettiest garden I had ever seen. Our plans for the day were to *mud* the sheet rock at the cabin in the morning and go fishing in the afternoon...but we worked in the garden instead. Charley sure needed a break from his normal work routine, because he had worked so hard for the past six weeks. We found that we were always pulled away to do other projects other than the ones that we needed to work on. Although we enjoyed all that we did, we were sometimes discouraged when we could not work consistently on our own projects. As much as Papaw enjoyed helping us with the cabin and the power line, he also wanted to get his garden taken care of as the need arose...which was most days throughout the spring and summer.

Papaw watered his garden from the nearby creek which kept everything growing well during the dry spells. He used an old lawn mower frame, put a pump on this frame, a draw pipe to the creek bed, attached a hose pipe to the pump and used that pump to get water to his garden. He used this pump for many years. (He always had a great garden because he spent a lot of time watering and tending to it...and a lot of prayer!)

We have worked in Papaw's garden quite a bit during the past couple of weeks. On Monday we picked, broke up, and canned 21 quarts of green beans; and on Thursday we put up 35 quarts and five pints of green beans. It was very hard work but enjoyable. In fact, we had been working so hard that while Papaw was cutting the tips of the green beans, he actually fell asleep with a paring knife in one hand and a green bean in his other hand. He looked so cute as he sat there...we just let him sleep.

(That would have been a great Kodak moment. Seems you never have a camera around when you need one!)

Monday, July 24, What a day! We were in the garden by seven o'clock this morning, and we worked until nine-thirty tonight. We canned fourteen quarts and four pints

Papaw loved working in his garden whether it was planting, gathering, or canning. Here he is preparing green beans for canning.

of green beans for a total of 100 quarts green beans canned this season. Wow! We also froze three pints of peas. Note: When we were in the garden so early, the vines and grass were covered with a heavy, wet dew. By the time we were finished picking in the garden, our clothes were soaking wet from the waist down. So, when we finished picking the green beans (and other vegetables) we would all change into dry clothes and then I would wash and dry our wet clothes while we processed the beans or other produce.

After we left Papaw's we went to the Mennonites and purchased 20 pounds of tomatoes for five dollars. We also bought three bell peppers and three yellow tomatoes for fifty cents. (We have been buying from a minister on Denson Road in Lawrence County who has a very nice family and is very fair with his prices.) We used the tomatoes and pepper in stewed tomatoes that we canned after we returned home from a day of canning at Papaw's.

Charley burned his arm today while we were canning. It was not serious but it was aggravating and the burn stung. We put some Foille ointment on the burn and that took away some of the pain and hopefully will prevent blistering. We were very tired after another long day! The low this morning at Papaw's was 51° with the high in the upper 80s.

Tuesday, July 25, Charley and Papaw pulled 1,155 ears of corn. Connie, Sandy and I put 30 quarts in the freezer and we gave away several hundred ears (we had corn up to our ears!). It was a very long and tiring day.

The weather was perfect. The low at Papaw's this morning was 48°, the high was upper 70s to low 80s. It was very cool and brisk with a soft wind blowing, which made shucking the corn very pleasant.

Wednesday, July 26, This morning I canned six pints of tomato juice and eight pints of little corn on the cob.

Charley and Papaw picked fifteen gallons of butter beans. We shelled most of them today and gave some away. We put eleven quarts in the freezer. Tomorrow we will finish shelling and freezing the butter beans and pick peas and green beans.

The weather was not as cool and pleasant today. At the trailer we had 1.4 inches of rain before we got home. Sure wish that we had gotten that on the garden.

I removed ten seed ticks off of me today. They sure do itch. I do NOT like ticks...but they sure think a lot of me!

Thursday, July 27, we were in the garden by seven o'clock. This is the fourth morning in a row that we have been there by seven (*Charley is **not** an early riser. These early mornings were very hard on him.*) We picked green beans, peas, okra and tomatoes. We broke up everything, canned the butter beans and peas and Connie cooked the green beans.

Connie also baked a one layer cake to eat with strawberries. They were delicious. It was good having Connie around because she not only cooked for us but washed up all the pots and pans that we used for shelling and canning. It was so nice to have someone else to cook and clean for a change.

You have heard the expression: "A man's work is from sun to sun, but a woman's work is never done." Well, I found that saying to be true. I was in the garden, kitchen, power line, cabin construction, field, or on the lake fishing on any given day. So, it was a great treat for me to have another woman around to share some of the load…even if it was only a day here and a day there.

It's Friday, July 28. What a day! Papaw, Connie, Charley and I went fishing. We decided that after all of the gardening that we had been doing that we were due a break. We arrived at Laurel Hill Lake at about 6:30 in the morning. Papaw and Connie arrived at 7:00. It was 6:45 that evening when we left for home.

We caught a total of 15 fish that weighed 42 pounds!! Charley and I went to a little cove that had some tree limbs in the water (and some shade). Connie and Papaw

stayed more toward the center of the lake. We had been fishing for just a few minutes when I hooked a big one (at least it felt like a big one!). Of course, Charley had to help me get the fish in the boat with a lot of work and a lot of prayer. He kept saying "This is a big fish! This is a big fish!"

We would almost get the fish to the dip net, and then it would dive under a tree branch. It seemed as though that fight went on for thirty minutes or more.

When we finally got that fish in the boat, we could not believe our eyes. Charley got out his fish scales to see how much it weighed…we were shocked! That catfish weighed eleven pounds! Later, Charley and I caught two more catfish that weighed five pounds and four pounds each. (Now, remember that Papaw was very competitive in everything he did. Even though he was a little jealous of our "catch," he was also very proud.)

According to the calendar it was not a good fishing day. We all laughed that we could not have stood it if it **had** been a good fishing day. We were all very tired, but we enjoyed our day (and we talked about that fishing trip for years). It was hard for me to believe that I had actually caught a 25 pound fish...whoops, I'm getting to be a true fisherman...not even home yet, and it's more than doubled in size!

On Saturday Charley and Papaw pulled 375 ears of corn.   That's a total of 1576 ears of corn this year. Connie, Sandy and I put eleven quarts of corn in the freezer. They did this for Charley and me to take home to our freezer. We were touched that they wanted to help us put some in our freezer…it will be good for our own family gatherings during the winter. *(Even though we could have taken any of the canned/frozen vegetables home with us, we hardly ever did so. Papaw loved to give the food to others and our pleasure came from the happiness he derived from being able to give.   However, the canned/frozen vegetables came in handy also, when we prepared meals at his house...which was more often than at our trailer.)*

Connie cooked breakfast for all of us. We had sausage, scrambled eggs, sliced tomatoes, gravy, biscuits and cantaloupe. It was all delicious. (We hardly ever ate a breakfast like this. We usually ate a Little Debbie Oatmeal Crème Pie on the run. Charley would drink a Mountain Dew, and I would drink milk or water.)

When we got home, we canned three pints of small corn on the cob, worked on a children's church program for Sunday, and did some odd jobs. It seemed as though we never stopped. Thank goodness for days of fishing to make the other days more tolerable.

Thursday, August 3, we were at Papaw's by seven o'clock to pick butter beans. We were able to put four pints in the freezer. Then we went to Waynesboro to get turkey livers to go fishing tomorrow.

On Friday, we went fishing: Papaw, Lewis (a friend of Papaw's from his church), Charley and me. We met at seven, however, it was so stormy looking with clouds and lightning that we did not get on the lake until about eight. As usual, we stayed about twelve hours. Boy was I tired. After the clouds passed over it turned out to be a beautiful day, but it was hot in the mid-90s and not a lot of breeze. Papaw caught four, Lewis caught three, I caught three, and Charley caught two. I caught the largest at five pounds, Charley caught two that weighed three pounds each. Papaw felt redeemed because he caught the most fish. Lewis took their catch of the day home with him. Charley and I brought ours with us. Our plans were to cook them for lunch the next day, but those plans changed.

It's Saturday and our plans for today were to sleep late and not do a lot of work, but Papaw called early because he wanted Charley to help disc the two spots where he wanted to sow wheat and clover. Paul also came down to help. Greg and his family were there along with Jen and Sandy. Jen brought pork chops and a pork roast and I cooked corn, mustard greens, fried potatoes, green beans and cornbread. Everything was delicious. We enjoyed the food and fellowship (we did not have a lot of time for fellowshipping with *our* projects in the woods).

Wednesday, August 16, we went to Papaw's where we picked four buckets (five gallons each) of green beans. We gave them all away as we had canned all the green beans that we needed for this year.

Charley took his tractor to pull the metal stakes out of the ground in the garden. Then he disked the garden so Papaw could plant his mustard greens and turnips. Something happened to Charley's tractor so it will have to be fixed...again!

On Thursday, while Charley worked on his tractor, Papaw and I mowed his yard. It took us over two hours, and Charley was nice enough to do the push mowing for us after he worked on his tractor. We are hoping that the tractor is fixed...and ready to go!

Tuesday, August 22, Papaw fertilized the upper place, the half-acre, and the bottom. His little trailer had a flat tire so he went to Hohenwald to get a new tire put on the wheel, and then I helped him put it back on the trailer. Some days you have to do what you have to do...no matter how hot it is!

September 18 – 22, We went to Gulf Shores with Connie and Wilma (see Family Activities for more details). While we were in Gulf Shores I called Papaw, morning and evening, to make sure that he was okay. One evening when I called him about six o'clock, he did not answer. It was not Wednesday, so he should not have been at church. *(Papaw hardly ever missed church on Sunday and Wednesday unless he was extremely sick, which was rare for him.)* Anyway as I was saying...I tried calling Papaw with no answer. I called Paul to see if he had talked to his dad, but he had not. Paul decided that he would go to Papaw's to check on him to see if he was okay. On the drive to Papaw's (Paul lived about 17 miles from Papaw's house), he saw Papaw's truck at the Oak Grove Methodist Church where there was a community-wide church meeting. When I talked to Papaw later that evening, he said that he had forgotten to tell me that he was going to the meeting.

A side note here: Papaw had a frequent tendency of slipping off from time to time without telling any of us. This made all of us worry about him, and make special trips just to check on him. He also would not hang up the phone properly, and we would get a busy signal, again causing one of us to go to his house to check on him. Because he lived alone, we were always concerned that he had fallen and gotten hurt (which he had done a few times but was never seriously hurt). His philosophy was that he was over 21 and did not have to check in with us…but it did not help our worrying. I think that sometimes he just needed a little special attention, and he knew just how to get it!

Tuesday, September 26, Papaw had to weld the exhaust pipe on Charley's tractor, and then Charley changed the oil and filter. After that, Charley finished bush hogging the upper place for Papaw. The tractor seemed to be working very well.

Wednesday, October 11, 2000, Charley took some rebar to his dad's for his dad to make some "chisels" to use to chip out the rock. He said that he got about six to eight inches more chipped out on one of the holes for the utility poles today. Both holes are now about 42 inches deep, but we need a minimum of 66 inches. Charley has built up some good muscles, but I am not sure that this is how he wanted to do that. Chipping rock is a very hard, strenuous job.

Papaw and I picked, stemmed, and put up sixteen pints of mustard greens. I then fixed lunch of fried chicken, gravy and biscuits. He and Charley really seemed to enjoy the meal (when the men enjoyed the meal it made all the effort worthwhile).

Friday, November 10, it is still too muddy to pull the wire so Charley and I went to Papaw's and put up mustard greens.

Charley headed to work on the power line.
Notice those muscles!

Charley and Papaw picked eight large stainless steel bowls of greens which yielded 25 pints of greens for the freezer. Charley then picked one large garbage bag of turnip greens and two large garbage bags of mustard greens for us to take home to put in our freezer. Those greens yielded 22 pints of mustard greens, 8 pints of tur- nip greens, and 10 pints of mustard and turnip greens mixed, all put in the freezer for a total of 65 pints. I am whipped!

The following list is a summation of what we canned during the gardening season of the year 2000. This list has not been altered in any way...it is exactly what we did...while we worked on the cabin, the power line, kept grandchildren, church activities and helped Papaw with his many, many other projects (including mowing about four acres of yard each week).

June 26	dug 21.75 bushels of potatoes
July 10	canned 21 quarts green beans
July 13	canned 35 quarts and 5 pints green beans (Mennonites)
July 14	froze 20 quarts silver queen corn (Mennonites)
July 17	froze 16 quarts silver queen corn (Mennonites)
July 20	canned 26 quarts green beans
July 20	canned 13 quarts stewed tomatoes
July 24	canned 14 quarts / 4 pints green beans
July 24	canned 14 quarts stewed tomatoes
July 24	canned 4 pints tomato juice
July 24	froze 3 pints of purple hull peas
July 25	pulled 1155 ears of corn (Papaw's) froze 30 quarts of corn
July 26	canned 6 pints tomato juice

July 26	canned 8 pints corn on the cob
July 26	froze 11 quarts butter beans (picked 15 gallons)
July 27	canned 3 pints pickled green tomatoes
July 27	froze 3 pints butter beans
July 27	froze 4 pints peas
July 29	froze 11 quarts corn (375 ears pulled)
July 31	froze 11 pints peas (picked 12 gallons)
August 1	canned 5 quarts stewed tomatoes
August 3	froze 4 pints butter beans
August 5	canned 21 pints of Salsa
August 7	canned 4 pints tomato juice
August 10	canned 14 pints extra hot picante sauce
August 16	canned 2 pints pickled okra
August 18	canned 2 pints pickled okra
August 20	canned 12 – ½ pints pickled green tomatoes
August 22	canned 1 pint pickled okra
August 29	canned 1 pint pickled okra
Sept. 13	canned 4 pints pickled banana peppers
October 11	froze 16 pints mustard greens
October 12	froze 20 pints mustard greens
Nov. 10	froze 47 pints mustard greens
Nov. 10	froze 10 pints mustard / turnip greens
Nov. 10	froze 8 pints mustard greens

Note: Green beans, corn, and peas were all shucked, broken, or hulled the same day as they were picked. As you can see...a lot of time was consumed by the garden. Even though we could not work on the cabin or power line during this time, the vegetables would come in handy during the winter. "Mennonites" means that we bought this produce from the Mennonites to can or put in <u>our</u> freezer at the trailer.

Charley paused in his power line work and cabin building to help Papaw and me with canning green beans.

Friday, November 17, 2000: I had cooked a pot of pinto beans yesterday, so I took them to Papaw's and fixed lunch for Papaw, Bud, Charley and me. Bud and Charley were working at the cabin, so I knew they would need a good hot meal about lunch time. I was busy working on other projects while I was cooking the beans, so the beans were "kinda" burned – Bad! But, some were salvageable, and we were able to have a good meal.

(Charley is always fussing at me for trying to do so many things at one time. Don't all women do more than one thing at a time? I think it is part of our genetics. Of course, if we women could not do three things at one time, then the men would have two things to do at one time…which is impossible!)

Thursday, November 23, 2000 was Thanksgiving Day, and it was also Paul and Jerry's birthdays. I baked two loaves of cranberry/orange bread, and Charley put a glaze on them to take to the family Thanksgiving meal. We went early to Papaw's so we could help Connie fix lunch. She had laryngitis and a cough so she did not feel very well. Sandy, Jen, Trisha, Ola, and Jeanne Bancroft brought in food. I will attempt to list the food we had: Turkey, two hams, mustard greens, butter beans, field peas, chicken and dressing, chicken and dumplings, mashed potatoes, sweet potato casserole, vegetables and dip, chicken casserole, fruit salad, macaroni and cheese, corn, cranberry sauce, and giblet gravy. Desserts were: pecan pies, coconut cake, applesauce stack cake, yellow cake with chocolate icing, oatmeal cookies, Connie's European cake, and cranberry/orange bread. There was also homemade biscuits, cornbread, and "Connie Bread" (her special sourdough bread). Everything was delicious.

There were 26 people at Papaw's house. We tried to make sure everything was cleaned up before we left. I washed all of the dishes after lunch. Judy, (Hal's wife), and Ola helped dry the dishes. (Have I mentioned that

Papaw did not have a dishwasher? All of the dishes had to be washed and dried by hand.) I was exhausted when the day was over. We are very blessed and have so much to be thankful for; and the gathering of family and friends makes us realize just how blessed we are.

On Monday, December 18, we took Papaw's book to him for his final approval. We have been working on "his book" for several weeks so he can give it to his five children for Christmas. He was very pleased with the results but did have a few last minute changes. He could hardly wait until Christmas to give it to them.

Wednesday, December 20, Charley got Papaw's book printed off for his brother and sisters, his dad, Bud, and one for himself. He just lacked the front covers and the genealogical section. A lot of work went into Papaw's book as we (and he) wanted it to be the perfect gift.

Thursday, December 21, Charley worked on Papaw's book most of the day. He designed the cover and finished the genealogical section. He has worked hard on the book and is very proud of the final outcome. We believe Papaw will be very proud of *"his"* book as well.

Saturday, December 23, we had Christmas at Papaw's. It was very busy. Connie had baked and cooked a massive amount of food and others brought food, as well. Charley and I helped her with the cooking, as did Jen. I think I washed all of the dishes…more than once as people came in to get a taste of this or that, or to get a glass of water. Charley helped clean up the kitchen after the meal. I don't think it would have ever gotten done if he had not helped.

Charley's brother and sisters were thrilled with the book that Papaw gave them. They were surprised at all the work and detail that had gone into the book. Charley and I had taken Papaw to Florence for the day during the summer. We took pictures of places of where he and Mamaw had lived, gone to school, worked, and gone to church. We then told Papaw's story in his words. Papaw was very pleased with the way *his* book turned out and so was everyone who received one. Although Papaw (and earlier Mamaw) always fussed when everyone gave them some small trinket (or nice gift), they were both like little kids as they tore into each package, being sure to publicly thank each giver before going to the next gift. But this particular Christmas Papaw was more focused on what he was giving – "*his book*" – than what he was getting.

On Monday, December 25, Christmas Day, Charley and I went to Papaw's. It would have been his and Mamaw's 63rd wedding anniversary. Charley helped Papaw work on the fuse box because fuses kept blowing. Charley wanted to re-wire it so he worked on that and got it fixed.

I finished cleaning the kitchen from Saturday night's gathering, cooked lunch for the three of us, and cleaned the kitchen, again. Then I un-decorated the Christmas tree and put everything away. Now I know that it seems to be way too soon to take down the Christmas tree – that

Sandy had just put up on the 23rd – but Papaw always liked for things to get back to normal as quickly as possible. After all, we were working on a power line, building a cabin, working on tractors…well, you get the picture. He didn't want his tree still standing as the next Christmas flew by!

Monday, January 1, 2001, we went to Papaw's to watch the Tennessee Vols football game with him and then I washed his bed clothes, and made up his bed. I put away the clothes that Trisha had folded yesterday. I also cleaned out the refrigerator of all the food left from Christmas, washed up all the dirty dishes from the refrigerator, cooked lunch and cleaned the kitchen. We had our traditional meal: hog jowl, black-eyed peas, slaw, and cornbread. Charley sliced and cooked the hog jowl. Everything was delicious and just what we needed to start the New Year in the right way.

Saturday, January 6, 2001, we fixed lunch at Papaw's today. We had fried potatoes, fried pork chops, gravy, biscuits, and slaw. Charley said it was my best gravy ever.

Yesterday I made vegetable soup with venison. Boy was it delicious! Papaw loved anything with deer meat in it, especially if it was a deer that he had killed.

On Saturday, January 20, we fried catfish and all the fixings for Papaw's 82nd birthday. All his children were there except for Jen, who lives in Mount Juliet. She was sick all night so she was unable to come to her dad's.

Monday, February 5, Papaw had decided earlier in the year that he wanted to get all of his property surveyed and deeded over to his five children. He said that they could start paying the taxes on the property. I just hope that he is feeling okay and not sick or anything. Sometimes he does not tell us everything. Charley went over all the papers with Papaw in preparation for the survey of the property.

On Thursday, February 8, we went to Papaw's to again go over the deeds in preparation for the survey. We stay at his house until two o'clock and then went to Lawrenceburg to pick up some supplies from the Lawrenceburg Power System.

Tuesday, February 20, Charley again worked on the survey. We went to Papaw's today where we ate chicken and dumplings and they sure were very good. Papaw is sick with a cold so hopefully the chicken and dumplings will help him to feel better.

Monday, March 5, Charley and Jack helped Kenneth Carroll, Land Surveyor, start the survey for Papaw's property. They got about two-thirds done today, and they plan to work again on Wednesday. Charley is tired tonight from all the walking.

On Wednesday, Charley did a lot of walking for the survey. He was the "lead" man, meaning that he walked ahead to flag points for the surveyor, then walked back to where the others were, only to re-walk the same steps again as they moved forward. He walked most of the property lines three times! And all of the land was up and down hills and hollows which many are very steep. Add to that the fact that he cannot hear when his back is turned to the others, or if he is more than ten feet from them, and that adds a lot of stress...and steps...for him. So he is not only physically exhausted but mentally exhausted as well.

On Thursday, the survey's outer perimeter was finished! The next step will be for the surveyor to "paper locate" the dividing points along this perimeter, to evenly divide the property. They then will have to physically pinpoint the corners in the field...which requires another survey of the perimeter plus a complete pinpointing of points along each lot's dividing lines.

On Monday, March 19, the full survey including lot divisions was completed! Now we can get back to working at the cabin. It took them all day to do the final lot line surveys.

Thursday, April 5, Papaw killed two turkeys today...with ONE shot! He came by to give us one and asked Charley to take it to Self's Market on Highway 64 to get it checked in. Papaw said property owners can kill a turkey without a stamp...and it worked. Charley did not have any problems getting the turkey checked in. Papaw could not believe that he had killed two turkeys. Hunting laws only allow one turkey per day and three turkeys per person per season. So, he could not tell anyone that he killed two with one shot. (We can share this story now because it happened so long ago...and I do not think they will be leaving a citation on his head stone.)

AMAZINGLY, it actually happened again another day. Papaw used a scope and as he pulled the trigger for the turkey that he had in his sights, another turkey stepped in line (or close) to the first turkey and the multi-shot load of his shotgun killed two turkeys with one shot. *(And, of course, the sentencing for accidently killing an extra turkey, and leaving it laying, is probably greater than accidentally killing a person!)*

Saturday, April 28, we planted in Papaw's garden today. He had turned and disked the garden, laid out the rows, and called and asked if we could plant it today. So we did. Connie was there and she helped, too. She also fixed lunch for us while we continued working in the garden. Before we finished the planting it started lightning, thundering and raining so we had to quit. When the rain stopped we went back and finished planting the seed that Papaw had gotten. The rain was good for the garden. It was also good for the flowers that we planted at the cabin.

Tuesday, May 1, Papaw got the remainder of the seed for his garden yesterday, and we finished planting the garden today. We planted cantaloupe and okra, and set out tomato plants. Just writing about this makes me hungry for fresh vegetables!

Thursday, May 10, Papaw, Lewis (a friend from his church), Charley and I went fishing at Laurel Hill Lake today. We went in our boat and Papaw and Lewis went in Papaw's boat. Charley caught five fish, I caught one, and Papaw and Lewis did not catch any. We had a great day. Well, Charley and I had a great day, Papaw was a little upset that he did not catch any fish (remember, he was very competitive). We gave all the fish to Lewis for him to eat for his supper. We got about a half-hour of rain while we were on the lake, but we kept fishing. We covered ourselves with ponchos and kept dry, although I never did warm up again after the rain. The temperature was in the 80s until it rained, and then it cooled off considerably. We were able to get in bed around 9:30... fishing is hard work!

Mid-May through Mid-June, mowing season had started. We helped Papaw mow his four acres several times within a few weeks. Of course, we were never able to do a job without maintenance on a piece of equipment.

One day when we tried to help Papaw mow his yard, both of his riding mowers broke down. One of the mowers had a belt that was broken, and the other one had the direct drive that controls the blades to break. So Papaw went to Waynesboro to get parts for the mowers. When he returned home, he and Charley fixed the mowers, and we finally finished with the mowing.

There was ongoing work in the garden as we had to hoe out the rows to keep out the weeds. Charley used the tiller, but Papaw and I used the hoes in the places where Charley could not reach with the tiller.

Thursday, June 28, we dug potatoes today. We recalled the old saying that "July rains will cause your potatoes to rot." We picked up thirty 5-gallon buckets of potatoes which converted to 19.5 bushels of potatoes.

It took us all day to dig the potatoes. First, we pulled the potato vines, and then we put the vines around the green beans and corn to use as mulch. After that we picked up the potatoes that came up with the vines. Charley used the tractor and potato plow to dig up the rest of the potatoes. He went over the rows several times to insure that we had gotten all of the potatoes. We used the 4-wheeler and Papaw's little trailer to take the buckets to the front yard where they were emptied and spread out in batches.

After all of the potatoes were in the front yard, we pulled the hose pipe around to the yard and began to wash the potatoes. We used large stainless steel bowls and filled them with water and washed each potato by hand. After they were all washed and air dried, we sorted them by size and put them in the potato bins in the barn. We worked on the potatoes for nine-and-a-half hours. We were exhausted!

We saw three snakes while we were digging the potatoes. Charley killed two of them and the other one got away. One of the snakes that Charley killed was a copperhead and the other was an Adder (spread-head like a cobra – probably non-poisonous but deadly with looks).

The copperhead is definitely poisonous. The snake that got away was a little ring snake. It is not poisonous or harmful, and it eats insects. That is four snakes that we have seen this spring and summer. I don't really care for snakes of any kind, at all!

On Thursday, July 5, we went to Papaw's where we picked, cut off tips, broke up, and canned fourteen quarts of green beans. They look very pretty. We started early this morning, and we were through canning by one o'clock.

Saturday, July 7, we helped Papaw mow his yard. Charley did all the push mowing while Papaw and I used the riding mowers. The heat index was around 100° and Charley got too hot while mowing. We cannot get an early start mowing the yard because the grass is too wet. So by the time we started mowing, it was really too hot to mow, but you "do what you gotta do."

Connie came in and cooked T-Bone steaks, baked potatoes, salad, and biscuits for lunch. She also made a yellow cake with chocolate icing for Charley's birthday (which was yesterday). The good meal, and cake, helped Charley to recover from the heat.

On Monday, July 9, we processed and canned 49 quarts of green beans (that is seven batches of canning). Thankfully we had two pressure cookers and we could cut the time in half by using both cookers at one time. We were in the garden by seven o'clock. We picked five 5-gallon buckets of green beans. We had a system. Charley,

Papaw and I picked, washed, tipped, and broke up
 enough beans to get enough to start one can-
ner. While I started the canning process (blanching, putting in jars and then in the pressure cooker), they continued to work on tip-
ping and breaking. I continued to break beans while the first batch was being processed, until we had enough to start the second batch. The three of us followed this process until all seven batches were finished. We barely took time for lunch! We finished about seven o'clock. It was a long, but productive day. We fell into bed at nine-
thirty.

On Thursday, July 12, we canned 30 quarts and 4 pints of green beans. At this time we have canned 102 quarts of green beans.

On Monday, July 16, we canned 28 quarts of green beans, plus we gave some green beans to Jeanne Ban-
croft, Papaw's neighbor. We also cooked a pot of green beans that should be good for several meals. Charley picked about one-half gallon of blueberries. Then he cleaned out a bunch of vines and undergrowth so the blueberries could grow better. (Note: The blueberries never did produce as well again after we cleaned out the undergrowth. According to Papaw we took away the natural mulch!)

Charley also disked the potato spot so Papaw could plant his mustard and turnip greens. We then went around the ridge and picked almost four gallons of blackberries. We canned 13 one-half pint jars of blackberry jelly and kept some out for a cobbler.

On Friday, July 20, Papaw and I put up 18 quarts of silver queen corn in the freezer. It took us most of the day. Charley mowed Papaw's yard and then came home and worked on our deck at the cabin.

On Wednesday, July 25, 2001, Papaw and I picked four 5-gallon buckets of green beans, and the vines are still hanging full for Saturday's picking. And on Thursday, July 26, Charley, Papaw and I picked nearly three 5-gallon buckets of butterbeans. We put 13 ½ quarts in the freezer. Charley also did the push mowing for Papaw's yard.

On Monday and Tuesday, we put 86 bags of corn in the freezer. Papaw, Sandy, Jack, Charley and I have worked diligently to get the corn put up. Monday we gathered 330 ears of corn and Tuesday we gathered 620 ears of corn. Even though we worked very hard, we really enjoyed the time that we all spent together. We were absolutely exhausted after these two days of work.

On Thursday, August 1, Papaw and I picked, shelled, and put up seven bags of purple hull peas. We then mowed the yard.

On Wednesday, August 15, Charley disked the garden spot today and then he worked on the county road near the Old Trace Drive. This drive is on the Laurel Hill Wildlife Reserve, and the county does not grade it. The LHWR does not keep their roads in top shape since most travel is 4-wheel drive, rough-terrain vehicles. But this section of road is our connection to the Natchez Trace, so we try to keep it in fairly good shape.

On Monday, August 20, Charley bush hogged two clover fields for Papaw and worked on the road going down the hill to the bottom.

On Wednesday, September 5, Papaw and I mowed all day. I even used the push mower. I actually thought that I was having a heart attack. My chest hurt, my legs were weak and my face was blood red. I had absolutely no energy. I also got about 50 tiny little seed ticks off of me (this is not a fish story...these figures are accurate!). Have I mentioned that I HATE ticks?! Eewww!

Saturday, September 8, Charley and I went to Papaw's where Charley sprayed the yard for ticks...too late, they were all on me! We both have gotten so many ticks off of us that he thought it would be a good idea to spray for them (I agreed!).

He and Papaw finished putting up the gutters. I folded Papaw's clothes and put those away and made his bed for him. I also cleaned the kitchen and dining room and swept and mopped the floors. Jen came down, and we both fixed lunch for all of us. Then we cleaned up the kitchen. It was good to spend some time with Jen as we have not seen her for a while.

The following list is what we processed during the canning season of 2001:

May 7	Canned 28 ½ half-pint jars strawberry preserves
May 11	4 quarts frozen strawberries
May 17	11 quarts frozen strawberries
June 28	Dug 19.5 bushels of potatoes
July 2	Canned 7 quarts green beans
July 5	Canned 14 quarts green beans
July 9	Canned 49 quarts green beans
July 12	Canned 30 quarts and 4 pints green beans
July 12	Canned 14 one-half pints jars blackberry jelly
July 16	Canned 28 quarts green beans
July 16	canned 13 one-half pints blackberry jelly
July 16	2 quarts frozen blackberries
July 17	18 quarts silver queen corn (frozen)
July 21	14 quarts green beans
July 21	Canned 16 pints peach pie filling
July 23	4 quarts frozen blueberries
July 24	25 quarts silver queen corn (frozen)
July 26	13 ½ quarts butterbeans (frozen)
July 28	Canned 19 pints picante sauce

July 28	Canned 10 pints pickled okra
July 28	Canned 7 quarts and 1 pint stewed tomatoes
July 28	Canned 5 pints tomato juice
July 30	30 quarts hickory king corn (frozen)
July 31	56 quarts hickory king corn (frozen)
August 2	7 quarts purple hull peas (frozen)
August 2	Canned 4 quarts and 1 pint stewed tomatoes
August 6	6 quarts purple hull peas (frozen)
August 6	3 quarts butterbeans frozen
August 7	Canned 4 quarts stewed tomatoes
August 14	Canned 23 jars pear jelly
August 17	Canned 17 pints apples
August 17	Canned 9 ½ pints apple jelly
August 20	Canned 15 ½ pints apples
August 20	Canned 26 one-half pint jars apple jelly
Sept. 20	Canned 16 one-half pint jars pear preserves
October 18	21 pints mustard greens frozen
October 19	10 pints turnip greens frozen

As mentioned later in Chapter 8, Charley started his job with the Mount Pleasant Power System effective September 1. Although we had moved to the Mount Pleasant area by September 28, I continued to go to Papaw's a couple times a week to help him with housework, mowing

Here I am with two canners on the stove!

and other odd jobs. We also continued to go to his house on most Saturdays to see him and visit with others, who came in to see Papaw.

Papaw and I missed seeing each other every day, but we talked by phone usually twice a day. I always wanted to check on him in the mornings to see what he planned to do that day, and again in the evenings to see how his day went.

When we first moved to Sandy Hook, we were concerned about leaving Papaw in the hollow by himself (of course, he had his neighbors, the Bancrofts. Jeanne often invited him in for a meal), but the Lord had plans. Paul, Charley's brother, retired shortly after Charley went back to work. Paul and Papaw were able to spend a lot of time together fishing, deer hunting, and bush hogging, disking the garden and other areas to sow seed and, of course, working on the tractor. (Papaw's Farmall tractor continues to reside in its place of prominence in the barn even today).

Paul worked some during the winter months when it was too cold to do anything outside, and then he would be off the rest of the year. We always felt that we had our time with Papaw, and now it was Paul's turn. Papaw was happy to spend the time with Paul, just as he was happy to spend the time with Charley and me.

We lost Papaw to a boating accident while fishing on March 19, 2004. He had lived a long and happy life, and we were blessed to have shared in a portion of his 85 years. He had always said that when he died, he wanted to be hunting, fishing, or in his garden…he got his wish. In fact, he had caught the only fish that day…a two pound bass! He had also told me only a week before the accident that he was ready to "go see 'the wife' " as he always called Mamaw. God honored his request yet again!

Kathy's note: Papaw and I had a great relationship. He was the father that I had not had since my father was killed in an automobile accident when I was eleven years old. I was able to do with Papaw what I wish that I could have done with my own Dad by helping him as a daughter…not a daughter-in-law. We were able to pick on each other and yet, be frank with each other as well. Papaw and I worked well together and, in quiet times, we discussed a lot of things with each other. He was a great confidante…something that I miss to this day.

CHAPTER 6
Family Activities

O ur two oldest grandchildren, Brittany and Brandon, stayed with us from Tuesday, August 3, 1999 through noon on Saturday, August 7. During their stay with us we picked blueberries and gathered, shucked and silked corn for preparing corn on the cob to put in the freezer. We played in Jack's Branch off the Natchez Trace, baked cookies, went to the Lewis County Museum, and the train depot. We also went to the Meriwether Lewis Park and played in the creek there, and on another day we had a picnic at David Crockett State Park where we fed the geese and rode paddleboats in the lake.

We went to Centerville and bought some Armstrong turnovers - Charley's favorite from his childhood. (There is a*n interesting note about Charley and his pies. The first time we visited Armstrong Pies after finding that they had relocated to Centerville, we purchased several pies and when Charley paid for them he gave them an extra dollar with this story: It seems that in Charley's early years the kids at school would run to the bakery, that was on the school property in Hohenwald, prior to getting on the school bus and purchase pies for the ride home. Charley would often accompany some of the other kids but seldom purchased the pies – Why? – he typically had no money.*

But on one occasion he was particularly hungry. The fresh hot pies were a dime and yesterday's pies were a nickel. The fresh pies were gathered up at each cooking vat by flavors, but the day-old pies were arranged at the exit door in a large wire tray by flavors. Charley waited for the baker to leave the area to get a fresh pie for one of the kids, and then he picked up one of his favorite pies from the day-old batch, slipped it under his shirt and headed for the bus. He ate his pie but could not enjoy it to its fullest, knowing that he had stolen it.

So, now some forty-five years after his theft, Charley was paying for his nickel pie – the only thing he ever recalled stealing. The attendants at the bakery amusingly debated whether to take the payment...or to call the local police and have Charley arrested!)

Actually the attendants loved the fact that he told them his story, and I am sure that they have told it to others many, many times over the years (and embellished it along the way).

We finished up the week with a catfish dinner with all the trimmings at Papaw's. We had a great time with the kids, and we tried to keep them busy, or rather, they kept us busy!

On Friday, August 13, 1999, when we returned home from running errands, we baked a strawberry pie, friendship bread, and a birthday cake for Geoff and Derek. Our two youngest sons were coming for lunch on Saturday to celebrate their birthdays. (Derek's birthday is on August 16 and Geoff's is on September 3 and we were celebrating their birthdays at the same time.)

The birthday cake was mine and Charley's first attempt at baking a cake from scratch and decorating. It was a yellow cake with white icing, blue trim and pink flowers. It looked beautiful.

For the birthday lunch we had T-bone steaks, salad, baked potatoes, and sourdough bread. We ate strawberry pie for dessert and the boys took the birthday cake home with them. *(Note: We found out about six months later that the cake was not edible. We had left something out in the ingredients that made it taste like lard...and there was no lard in it...must have been a Friday the 13th thing.)*

After the boys left we went to the cabin site, which was our first visit since the dozer work (See Chapter 2).

On Saturday, September 4, we took Sully to the veterinarian's to stay for a few days while we were out of town. We went back home to do laundry and to pack for our trip to Chattanooga with Pat and Jerry for the Labor Day weekend.

We went to Scottsboro, Alabama for their annual yard sales/flea market. We then went on to Chattanooga where we scoured several antique shops. We stayed at the Chattanooga Choo Choo on Sunday night. Everybody had a great time, and the break was good for us.

Our fourth grandchild, Abigail Mae Gandy was born on Tuesday, September 20, 1999. We went to Columbia to see the baby, and we brought big brother, Chris, home with us so he could stay while his parents were at the hospital.

We had to buy a few toys for him as we did not have

anything for him to play with at the trailer. Chris enjoyed playing with our dog, Sully, and would share Sully's cage as they played together, and taking turns getting in the cage. *(Note: We did not put Chris in Sully's cage. We found him curled up in the cage barking and whining like a little puppy dog. He was so cute acting like he was a puppy. Sully was not sure he wanted to share his cage with this "new puppy".)* Chris slept in the bedroom with us, and we had to lock the bedroom door so that he could not slip out while we were sleeping. Chris had a tendency to venture out on his own when no one was watching...a very independent young lad!

Our trailer was surrounded by a pasture that housed cows and horses. With Chris's fascination with the livestock at three years old, we had to watch him carefully so that he did not sneak out to the pasture and get hurt.

One particular morning I woke up feeling someone staring at me. When I opened my eyes, there stood Chris beside the bed. When he saw my eyes open, he threw up his arms and sadly exclaimed, "I can't go nowhere!"

I could not help but laugh at the seriousness of his comment. I got up and Chris and I went outside to see the horses. We took Chris home to Hohenwald on Wednesday.

December 18, 1999, we had Christmas with the kids and their families and a church program that night, so we did not work that day – let me clarify: we did not work at the cabin. We even had to take some days off to do some Christmas shopping. The month of December had been very hectic. It rained on the 21st so Charley and I went to Papaw's to clean house for him before Christmas.

June 26 thru June 30, 2000, Brittany and Brandon spent the week with us. On Monday, we dug potatoes at Papaw's. They worked very hard and they loved driving the 4-wheeler back and forth with the potatoes. About midday, Brandon, who was four years old, said, "Mamaw, I'm tired of digging potatoes. When are we going to have some fun?" Little did he realize that our 'fun' was using the 4-wheeler while we worked!

Our work in the potato patch started about nine o'clock, and we finished about seven-thirty that evening. Everyone was exhausted, but we yielded 21.75 bushels of potatoes. The rest of the week was spent doing things that they enjoyed: played in the creek, went on a picnic, visited a museum in Hohenwald, and baked cookies. We had a lot of fun with them…but I am not so sure that they got the gist of the "fun" of digging potatoes.

July 6, 2000, today is Charley's 53rd birthday. We went to Chattanooga for the annual church Camp Meeting, where we stayed at the Chattanooga Marriott. Doug and Shirley (my brother and sister-in-law) were there (they live in Memphis where they pastor at Family Tabernacle, a Church of God). We were very excited to see them, as it had been over two years since we had been together. On Friday the four of us ate lunch together, and then went on a train ride. We had a lot of fun.

The camp meeting was good, too, as we learned helpful hints to assist us with teaching classes and working with children's church.

On Wednesday, August 16, Derek turned 21 years old. Hard to believe that my baby is 21…that sure makes me feel old!

On Friday, after working on digging another hole, we went to Papaw's to gather the okra. Afterward we went to Lawrenceburg to get cake and fixings for the catfish lunch for Bud's birthday on Saturday. When we got home, we made slaw, did the second step on the pickled green tomatoes, fixed two pints of okra, and Charley worked on thawing the fish for cooking. We had another busy day.

Saturday, August 19, we cooked catfish and all the fixings at Papaw's for Bud's birthday. He was very surprised, and he thoroughly enjoyed his birthday cake. I wondered if this was his first birthday cake ever. Bud had been so good to help us that we wanted to do something special for him. The house was full of family to help Bud celebrate.

Today is Sunday, September 3, 2000 – Geoff's 26th birthday. Did I mention earlier that I was getting old? Our children are not children anymore…they are adults with responsibilities of their own.

Pat wanted us to take her four kittens that are four months old, but we could not catch them. She called tonight and she had caught two of them. She had put a long rope on Little Mister's cage and she was watching the cage when two of the kittens and the mama cat walked in. She pulled the rope and closed the door. She could not believe that it was that easy. She and Jerry are supposed to bring them over tomorrow.

On Monday, September 4, 2000, Labor Day, Charley and I went fishing. We each caught five fish which was good, because that is the limit at Laurel Hill Lake. It was wild. I had caught two fish and by 1:30 we went to the "hollow" where I caught the eleven-pounder last month. We started out by me getting a bite and it felt like a big one. I just knew that I had another 25 pounder...I mean, 11 pounder! Charley caught two fish and then my anchor gave way and the boat swung around – we ended up tying off to a tree and the fish started biting.

Charley and I each caught three fish making the limit caught for the day. We fished for another thirty minutes, had a few good bites, but did not catch any more. Let me add that when, and if, we catch any fish above the limit, we cull the smaller fish and keep the larger one. The fine for having too many in the basket or stringer would not be worth the risk, or jail time.

Pat and Jerry brought the two kittens which we named Lizzy and Fluffy. They ran under the trailer and as of yet they have not come out. Perhaps they will come out tomorrow when they are hungry.

On Saturday, September 9, 2000, we went to the Aday family reunion in Russellville, Alabama. Charley was able to get some names that he needed for his genealogy research. We had a lot of fun and we met several "kin folk" and enjoyed some good food.

After the reunion we went through a double wide-trailer that had cedar siding that resembled logs. It was really nice and it had a lot of space. I especially liked the kitchen and the master bath. I was about ready to place my order for one, just so that we could get moved, but a double-wide was not the plan. We were to build our own cabin. Well, a woman can dream, can't she?

We saw Lizzy the kitten tonight. She came up on the deck to eat some food. As soon as she saw me, she ran off. We have not seen Fluffy. We do not know if he is still here or not. We will see.

It was a very humid day, the kind of day where you could hardly breathe. Temperature was in the low 80s. It did rain a little at the reunion but not very much. Just enough to make the air more sultry.

Friday, September 22, we spent this week in Gulf Shores, Alabama with Connie and Wilma (a life-long friend of the Gandy family). We had a very good week and lots of good food. We ate at Lambert's Café (Home of the Throwed Rolls) in Foley, Alabama on our way to Gulf Shores.

We walked on the beach Monday after we got there. On Tuesday we went back to the beach after we went grocery shopping. Charley and I put on a lot of Hawaiian Tropic 50 SPF sunscreen, but we "cooked." His legs were very red from the edge of his swim trunks to his toes, while the upper parts of my legs were red. It was very painful for both of us, and we were miserable for the rest of the week. Connie and Wilma used Coppertone 30 SPF and looked as if they had not even been in the sun.

On Wednesday, Connie, Charley and I went to Dauphin's Island by ferry and we also took a tour of Fort Morgan. It was a lot of fun and very relaxing, except for our sunburns. We had to stay inside on the ferry because the slightest hint of sun on our legs caused us to feel as though our legs were on fire.

On Wednesday the ocean was beginning to get more turbulent from Hurricane Helen that was out in the gulf.

By mid-afternoon Thursday, the wind was causing the gulf water to be extremely rough. There were red flags out indicating no swimming or surfing allowed.

Connie got up early and went to the beach. When she came back to the room, she cooked breakfast for all of us. Charley and I did not go to the beach that morning, but we walked over to the beach later that day during a break in the rain.

This morning (Friday) we drove to the beach before we left for home. It was really something to see. The water was approaching the beach so fast that it was coming all the way up to the buildings and splashing against the sides of them. The waves were capping 8 to 10 feet above the water level. It was a tremendous sight and the sound was deafening. The water was very turbulent. We were glad that we left before the storm hit the coast line in full force. We drove home with the rain chasing us most of the way!

Connie paid for the condo for the week through her timeshare plan. It was a wonderful week for us. The break did our bodies and minds good (well, except for the sunburned legs). We had not planned to take a vacation at this time, but when Connie asked us to go, we felt like the break would be good for us.

Tuesday, October 31, we are in the Smokies! Connie had a vacation package and she wanted someone to go with her. (Isn't that just like God? We were wishing that we could go to the mountains and here we are!) The drive was beautiful with the gorgeous fall leaves in full splendor.

Today we slept in. Connie cooked breakfast, and then we went to Cades Cove, which is an eleven mile loop. It was a glorious drive...again with all of the fall leaves and colors being so magnificent. While we were in Cades Cove, we saw five bears: three grown bears and two cubs. Charley got real close to the bears...I was afraid for him, but he was very daring. The largest bear – Papa Bear – wandered on over the hill while we watched. We took pictures of the other four.

Charley decided that he would go to the crest of the hill and see if he could see the Papa Bear. He topped the hill and was looking everywhere for the bear. Finally, he glanced up at the large tree that he was standing next to, and the Papa Bear was about ten feet above his head!

Needless to say that he did not pause for that Kodak moment! He was afraid that it might become a Kodiak moment! I did not know that he had that much energy left in him after all our power line work...but somehow I think he suddenly became re-motivated!

It was exciting to see all of the bears. We got a lot of great pictures. It took several hours for the tour, but it was worth it.

Wednesday, November 1 thru Friday, November 3, we went to Cherokee, NC to see the Indian Village, but it was closed for the season. So we went back to the Indian museum, where we enjoyed the history of the Indians.

We saw a bear alongside the road on the way back over the mountain. That makes six bears that we have seen this week. We also rode through "Roaring Fork" trails on our way back where we thought that we might see a bear or two, but we did not see any.

On Thursday we went to Cosby to show Connie the McMillan house. Rev. Anderson McMillan was the great-great grandfather of Charley, Connie and their siblings. The house had about fallen in completely. It was so sad to see the house let go like that, but it had not been lived in for many years. *(Charley and I had been at the house the year before and met one of the descendants of Mr. McMillan. He gave us a tour of the house, and it was amazing to see all of the antiques that were left in the house. The house was two-story with a colonial front. The young man explained to us that there was no one to live in the house, and that was the cause of the condition of the house. The water supply was gravity-fed from a mountain stream and was fed to the kitchen sink where it flowed continuously. Too bad that we could not have moved that house, and its contents, to the home place!).*

We could not get out of the van because of all the smoke in the area due to a forest fire that had been burning for a few days. Hopefully it will be put out soon as the fire is very close to Dollywood.

We "shopped till we dropped" today. Connie was able to get quite a few things for her "Country Store" for

Christmas. I know the kids will love everything that she has gotten for her store.

We go home tomorrow. The week has gone so fast, yet I am ready to go back. It will be good to get back to work. I am sure that both of us have put on weight this week from all of the eating we have been doing. Connie is a great cook, and we always look forward to her meals. Charley and I both needed to gain some weight as we have lost more than we needed to lose. Charley looks as though he has re-gained some of his strength and energy.

It is so hard to believe that a couple of weeks ago I was praying for a trip to the mountains...and He provided one for us. God is good...all the time.

Friday, we came home. We stopped at the Lodge Cast Iron outlet store today and bought two square skillets for less than $20 each. I saw one at an antique store for $40, so we really got a bargain. The square skillet is great for cooking cornbread as the corner pieces are so good with the extra crisp crust – and butter! *(But square cornbread does not fit round plates...so one thing leads to another...but we finally found square plates!)*

We got home about 5:30 tonight. On our way home we went by Pat's office (in Spring Hill) to see her, and then we went to her house to pick up Sully. Jerry was at home so we visited with him for a few minutes.

Greg and his family are spending the night at the cabin tonight so they can get an early start for deer hunting in the morning. Greg says there are a lot of wasps in the cabin, but there are some open areas that allow the wasps to get inside. They are using the mattresses with their sleeping bags on top. I am supposed to call Greg by 4:15 in the morning so they can get up and have an early start for hunting. They are our first "guests" to sleep over, and we aren't even there!

Friday, November 17, 2000: (Greg turned 32 years old on November 13.) Greg came over tonight. He was on his way to Papaw's to spend the night with him so he could go deer hunting in the morning. I fixed grilled cheese sandwiches and soup for supper. It wasn't much of a supper, but it was filling.

Saturday, November 25, Charley and I went to Pat and Jerry's for Jerry's birthday. We cooked a catfish and chicken supper for them, Jerri Ann, Bobby, and Nicole. It was very good, even though Pat and I forgot to put out the slaw. Oh well, you can't think of everything.

On Tuesday, December 5, Derek called to say that he wanted his bed that we were using. Unfortunately, we have so much going on that we cannot take it to him. The church bazaar is on Saturday (See Chapter 7) and we still have lots to do in preparation for that.

Thursday, December 7, Derek and two friends (Will and Jeffrey) came and got his bed. We gave them chili for supper and some fudge that we had made earlier in the day. When Jeffrey took a bite of the peanut butter fudge, he said, "That's the bomb!" He said it was the best fudge he had ever tasted. He wanted to know how to make it for his mom. *(We used a recipe that Derek had written out several years ago on a small piece of paper. He used the recipe in a required Home Economics class. The Fantasy Fudge recipe was on the back of a Kraft Marshmallow Cream jar. We continue to use that same recipe today with different variations.)*

Charley went to the cabin earlier today and got the bed that I had when I was a child. Mama and Daddy bought bunk beds for Pat and me when we were about nine or ten years old. I hope I don't fall off...Derek's bed was a queen size and I am accustomed to more space. Let me explain that Charley and I slept in separate beds because we worked so hard during the day that we rested better at night by sleeping alone. I will admit, though, that there was a path between the two beds.

On Saturday, December 16, we had Christmas with the boys and their families. We met at Catfish Dock in Lawrenceburg, and everyone ordered what they wanted to eat from the menu. It was really nice for everybody, especially me, as we had been so busy that I had not had time to prepare a Christmas meal. *(Even though it was nice to not have to cook, I will not go to a restaurant for our Christmas again, even if I have to get off my sick bed to fix a meal! But the trailer was so full of our things, that we would have had to eat in shifts.)*

Tuesday, December 26, we met Greg in Lawrenceburg to get Brittany and Brandon for a few days while school was out. On the way home we stopped at a barn that has miniature horses. We saw the owner outside and asked if the kids could go in and see the horses. He agreed, and the kids thought the horses were so cute. We all enjoyed seeing them up close. They were not even as tall as the kids.

Brandon always said that he wanted to be a veterinarian someday, and he talked about those horses during their whole visit with us. *(Note: Unfortunately, Brandon developed allergies as he grew up. And one of the things that he is allergic to? Horses. He starts college in the fall of 2014 where he plans to major in agriculture business.)*

On Friday, December 29, we met Greg to take Brittany and Brandon home. We had a good time with them during their visit, but it is now time to get back to work on our projects (and Papaw's).

Wednesday, January 17, 2001, was our 16th wedding anniversary. We went to Florence for the day where we went to Sam's Club and Wal-Mart to get supplies for the Sweetheart Banquet (See Chapter 7). Then we went to Lowe's to get a few things for the cabin. We had a nice anniversary meal at Ryan's Steakhouse (Happy Anniversary, Dear!) We really enjoyed our day together even if we did have to run a lot of errands.

On Sunday, January 21, 2001, we went to church this morning. Then Charley pulled a fast one on me. He had suggested that we eat out in Lawrenceburg, but then he decided that we would go to Lynnville to eat at the Iron Horse Restaurant.

As we neared Apple Hill Road where I grew up in Giles County, he suggested that we drive by the home place. My brother, Don, and his wife, Melody, own the property now, and they have built a very nice house there.

When we got to the house I noticed several cars in the driveway but I did not think too much about it. Then when Charley pulled into the driveway I knew something was up. Pat, Jerri Ann, and Melody had put together a 50th birthday party for me. It was so much fun and I got some pretty neat 50s gifts along with some nice gifts. It was a great surprise!

Yesterday (Saturday), Connie gave me a large vanilla scented candle and a long t-shirt gown that she had gotten in Gatlinburg. Sandy gave me a blue sweatshirt with a white collar and a spring scene on it. Papaw made sure that everybody sang "Happy Birthday" to me and not just to him, since his birthday is the 21st.

I have had a very good birthday already, and my birthday is not until tomorrow! Charley is always accusing me of stretching my birthday for the whole month of January...and somehow I do!

Monday, January 22, today is my 50th birthday. I have had a good day. Charley brought me breakfast in bed. I stayed home today and took all my birthday presents out of the van from yesterday's celebration, and made thank-you cards to send out. Charley grilled steaks for our supper, and we took one to our neighbor, Jay, who lives across the road.

Overall I have had a great day. Charley gave me a beautiful card and a brass bell with "Titanic 1912" on it. I love the gifts and everything he has done to make my birthday special.

On Sunday, March 11, Pat and Jerry helped us at the cabin all afternoon. When we returned to the trailer, we fixed a couple of small pizzas for supper. Jerry did not care for pizza, so Pat fixed him a ham sandwich. It sure wasn't much of a supper after all their hard work, but everyone was too tired to cook. Pat and Jerry sure have helped us a lot. We could not have gotten so much done without them.

Pat helped us when we moved to the cabin on March 29, 2001. Read more about this in Chapter 3.

Sunday, April 8, after church we went to Pat and Jerry's and got the mantle that he gave us (that was built in the 1840s) and a cherry drop-leaf table that she is letting us borrow until we can get a small table and chairs for our dining area. We also looked at a metal storage building that they are not using. If the building works for us, Jerry is going to give it to us. It will be very useful to store some of our things that we don't want left out in the weather.

On Thursday, April 19, we went to Pat's and got some Chestnut and Poplar boards that Jerry had given Charles. We also got the 8' x 10' metal storage building that they gave us. It needs to be painted and a little work on the doors, and then we will be able to store some things in it. We are thrilled to get it.

I cannot believe that the two of us loaded that building. Charley used two jacks to jack up where we could put blocks under it. He jacked up one side at a time. Each time he jacked it up, I put a block under the building. Then we would move to the other side and repeat the process. We did this procedure until we had the building high enough that we could back the trailer under the building, letting the building rest on the rails of the trailer.

We had to bring the building home by going north on Highway 31, then across Kerr Hill Road to Campbellsville through Liberty Hill, Ethridge, Center, over to Highway 64 then to Brush Creek and home (all back roads). It was a longer route but less traffic to have to maneuver through. Of course we had to avoid the Natchez Trace as it is illegal to haul anything except recreational vehicles and equipment on the Trace. I don't think we could have convinced a ranger that the building would be used for recreational purposes. It was not worth the fine to take the risk of traveling on the Trace.

When we got home, we had to remove the building from the trailer. We did that by jacking up the building, putting blocks under each corner (the corners hung over the rails of the trailer). When we got the building higher than the trailer, we pulled the trailer out from under the building. We then used the tractor, with its 3-point lift boom, to move the building to the spot where we want the building to set. It took us nearly five hours to unload and get the building where we wanted it, but it was worth the effort. We still need to level the building and do some repair work. It was after seven o'clock when we quit for the night, and then I cooked supper.

Charley pulled his shoulder during the process of moving the building, and he is in a lot of pain tonight. I'm hoping that he will feel better after a good night's rest.

On Friday, May 11, 2001, we bought fifteen quarts of strawberries: ten for Connie and five for us. We mashed and froze all of ours except enough for two pies. Charley and I worked in the yard. He cut down quite a bit of undergrowth around the cabin and I cleaned out around the flowers in the circle. Everything looks so much better.

We put our new bed coverings on our beds. They make the room look so much better with all of the colors, and they match the border around the ceiling very well. Charley cleaned up the concrete pad and picked up all the tools from around the tree. He put everything in and around the storage building. The inside and outside of the cabin have never looked better.

Sunday, May 13, 2001 – Mother's Day: Geoff and Derek came to eat lunch with us today. I don't mind cooking on Mother's Day when I know that I will get to spend time with the boys. This was the first time for Geoff and Derek to see our new home, and they were impressed with what we have done. However, I believe that our woods are too remote for them. (They enjoy the conveniences of living close to town...pizza delivery! You don't get pizza delivered in this neck of the woods...we are too remote for that!)

On Friday, May 18, we worked most of the day preparing for our trip to the mountains with Pat and Jerry. We also went to Papaw's and helped him with a few chores.

Sunday, May 27, while we were on our trip to the mountains, Geoff and Kelley let us know that they are getting married on June 15. They want to have an outside wedding with a Hawaiian theme. Jerri Ann is going to let them have the ceremony in her backyard. She and Kelley will do the planning and buy what they need. They have some great ideas so it will be a beautiful ceremony. We have a lot to do in the next two weeks.

Sully stayed with Bud and Ola while we were gone. They spoiled him rotten, and he had a great time... and so did they. According to Ola, Bud and Sully took lots of naps on the couch.

On Tuesday, May 29, Charley and I got our outfits for Geoff's wedding. I got a long red dress with purple splashes, and Charley got a Hawaiian print shirt.

On Tuesday, June 5, I went to Lawrenceburg to order the wedding cake for Geoff and Kelley's wedding. Kroger does not do wedding cakes anymore, and I did not like what Wal-Mart had to offer. The cakes were also very expensive.

Thursday, June 7, we went to Kroger and ordered the cakes for the wedding. Since Kelley did not want a traditional wedding cake, Kroger was able to make the cake for the wedding. The flowers on the cake will be Hawaiian themed in color and design. The lady at the bakery was very helpful in suggesting the type of flowers for the cake.

Saturday, June 16, what a week! On Wednesday I did what most women do before a big event...I had my hair colored. I have been going to the same woman for the past two years, and we always use the same color. But not this time!

She mixed up ash blonde instead of a light blonde. (She had picked up the wrong bottle!) My hair turned green! Not even a pretty shade of green. I never use any color with ash in it. I told her that I thought the color was wrong, but she assured me that it was the correct color.

After she dried and styled my hair, I went out to my vehicle, sat there a couple of minutes, and went back inside. I told her that my hair had a gray/green look to it (it looked much worse in the sunlight), and that she would have to fix it. So she put a light blonde color on my hair, but it did not lighten the color very much. It wasn't too bad, but not the color I wanted (or paid for!). I would have preferred it to be lighter. Thank goodness I had planned to wear a small hat for the wedding.

While I was in town I bought the fruit for the wedding. (When you live as far from town as we do, you have to make every trip count.)

Charley and Papaw had planned to go fishing on Thursday but it was too windy. So we changed our plans. We went to Columbia to visit Jerry in the hospital (explanation to follow). Then we came home and cut up the fruit and cheese for the wedding.

Friday, June 15, 2001, Wedding Day! We went to Kroger's in Lawrenceburg to get the cakes. Then we took the canopy and boxes of supplies to Jerri Ann's and put them in her garage. We took the coolers of fruit and our clothes to Pat's house.

After that we went to BI-LO in Pulaski to get the arches that we had rented for the wedding. There were two of them, and we could not get both of them in the van so we had to take one to Jerri Ann's, and then go back to Pulaski to get the second one (two – 16-mile round trips).

While we were in town we ate a meal at KFC, which turned out to be a good thing because we never had another opportunity to eat until the reception later that evening.

Geoff, Kelley, Sheila (Kelley's Mom) and Charles and I went to Jerri Ann's to help set up for the wedding. Bobby and Nicole came in to help, too. Before we could get a whole lot done it began to rain. Then it stopped raining...and started again. We were very worried as this was an outdoor wedding! Finally we were able to get the canopy up and put two tables under the canopy. Then we all left because it was raining too hard to do anything else.

Charley and I went to Pat's where he took a nap, while I showered and fixed my hair and makeup. I also washed Pat's dishes, folded clothes that were in the dryer, and made her bed so that everything would be in order when she and Jerry came home from the hospital.

While we were at Pat's, Jerri Ann fixed bouquets of flowers and decorations and filled up the balloons with helium. By the time we returned to her house, she had decorated both tables... a net and sea shells on one table, and pineapple and coconuts on the other table. We could hardly believe the transformation that occurred in the short time that we were gone.

Pam Gandy, Melody Graham, and Brenda Graves were the servers, and they did a fantastic job. They had to set out the food and make the fruit baskets. (Charley had cut out two watermelons to look like baskets and when they were filled with fruit they looked beautiful.)

Everything looked amazing! Jerri Ann did an outstanding job of decorating and planning the wedding. Geoff and Kelley's wedding was exquisite! The ceremony was simple, yet elegant. Kelley wanted a Hawaiian theme, and it was perfect. The colors were bright and beautiful. Jerri Ann had rented double arches that were strung with little white lights, and with the wedding at dusk, the lights were perfect.

The cake was awesome and delicious. We had Kroger to make a one-half sheet cake and put a six inch round cake on the left corner. It was decorated with orange and red around the top edges. Green scallops were on the side with red and orange flowers on the top. The rich colors were so vibrant against the white icing. The groom's cake was chocolate on chocolate with purple flowers. Both cakes had palm trees on top. The white cake had bells and wedding rings as decorations. Kroger did an excellent job.

Kelley wore a red dress with pink flowers. Geoff wore a Hawaiian themed shirt and shorts, and both of them were barefoot. It was cute.

Doug came from Memphis to perform the ceremony. He did a very good job, and it was a short ceremony.

There was only one glitch. Pat and Jerry were unable to be at the wedding because Jerry was in the hospital. Jerry had had a light heart attack on Wednesday, and they were at Maury Regional Hospital in Columbia. He was scheduled for surgery at St. Thomas Hospital in Nashville on Monday (June 18) where he would be having stents implanted. Bobby called Pat right before the wedding started and he put the call on speaker so that she and Jerry could hear the vows being exchanged.

We received a lot of compliments on the wedding and reception. Everyone said it was a perfect setting. The rain had moved out, and the evening was perfect.

We are very tired this Saturday morning and glad that the event is over.

Tuesday, June 19, Jerry came home from the hospital today. He was taken to St. Thomas by ambulance on Monday. He had two blockages…one at 90% and the other was 80%. The doctor at St. Thomas said he was lucky he made the trip to Nashville. (His doctor in Columbia told Pat before the ambulance left that he would be surprised if Jerry made it to Nashville). Fortunately, they let Pat ride with him in the ambulance.

When we arrived at St. Thomas the morning of the procedure, Melody and Jerri Ann were already there. They had driven Pat's van up from Columbia so she and Jerry would have a way home. After the surgery, which was successful, we took Melody back to Columbia so she could get her car. We returned home about nine o'clock.

On Friday, June 22, we got Geoff's wedding pictures. They are awesome. I cannot wait to give them to Geoff and Kelley. We also sent thank you cards to everyone who helped with the wedding.

Sunday, August 5, what a nightmare! Pat called about 10:30 p.m. on Friday (August 3, 2001) to tell us that Jerry had died. We could not understand what was happening. Jerry had been doing so well since he had had the stents put in his heart (six weeks ago). In fact, he went back to work last week. It appeared that he had a heart attack and died at home. The funeral was today. It has been a hard weekend for everyone, but especially for

Pat, Jerri Ann, Bobby and Melody. (Jerry was Melody's brother. Melody is married to our brother, Don.) Jerry is the first of us to pass away. He was the oldest of all of us (57), and everyone relied on him for everything. He was the person we all went to when we needed technical advice or just a friend.

Sunday, August 12, it has been a busy week. We had the interview for our mortgages on Wednesday. We went by the new house in Sandy Hook for a few minutes. (See Chapter 8.)

On Friday we took Brittany, Brandon, Chris and Abby to Chuck E. Cheese in Florence. It rained all day and the drive was terrible, but we had a great time with the grandchildren.

Charley and I spent the night with Pat on Friday night. Charley helped Bobby and Jerri Ann put the electricity to an above-ground pool that they had bought.

Saturday, August 24, today we worked on Pat's screened-in porch adding the finishing touches. After we finished the porch we went to Jerri Ann's to swim for a couple of hours.

Pat, Charley and I then went to help Derek move (he was moving to a different location). Even though Geoff, Kelley, and Mack were helping him, he would not have gotten it all done if we had not shown up. The high temperature was 102° today...in the shade! That pool felt very good.

Monday, September 3, 2001 (Labor Day): Today is Geoff's 27th birthday. Yesterday we played hooky from church and went to Florence. We very rarely skip church, but we needed a day off. It actually rained all day again today (that's what we get for skipping church).

While we were in Florence we went to Books-A-Million, Sam's Club, Lowe's, and a few antique stores and ate lunch at O'Charley's. We really enjoyed our day.

Today (Monday) we met Greg, Brittany, Brandon, Chris, and Abby at Pizza Hut in Lawrenceburg for lunch. Then we went to Pulaski to Flatrock Discount Furniture to do some looking around.

While we were at the furniture store, we ordered a bedroom suite; bought a computer roll-top desk; mattress and box-springs for the bed; and a mirror. Charley also bought me a large painting of Scarlett O'Hara from "Gone With The Wind." I absolutely love it. We paid too much for it, but it will look great in our living room. (I love anything that relates to "Gone With The Wind." Jerry had found a book that was the motion picture edition several years ago in an abandoned house, and he gave it to me earlier this year because he knew how much I loved "Gone With The Wind" paraphernalia.)

We went to Pat's for a few minutes and then met Geoff and Kelley at Shoney's in Lawrenceburg for his birthday.

Charley started his new job at the Mount Pleasant Power System on September 4, 2001. (He was hired in as chief engineer and became general manager on July 1, 2002, when the former GM retired)

I hope everything works out as well as it appears. We have enjoyed our adventure of the cabin and power line, but the Lord saw the big picture of our financial situation. After the entire ordeal that delayed our Bowling Green house sale; the delay of getting our cabin and power line completed; and all the over-runs of the "once-in-a-lifetime" adventure that changed with each unanticipated twist of fate, the big picture definitely changed.

The amazing thing is that throughout this entire process, our financial situation never really got completely out-of-hand...but definitely could use some relief. And so, through Divine intervention, we were able to finance our new Sandy Hook home on one mortgage, and finance our Cabin over-run on another mortgage – both at unbelievably low interest rates.

Chris and Sully having playtime <u>outside</u> of the cage!

Our Family – Christmas 2013

Chapter 7
Church Activities

W hen Charley and I first moved back to the area, we began looking for a church. We have always been involved in church work, and this part of our life would not be any different. Our first Sunday in the trailer, and each week following – through mid-August – found us visiting area churches and "trying them on" as to what we received, and what we could contribute to the congregations. On August 15, 1999, we attended church at Center Grove Church of God and felt that this was the place we were meant to be.

I did not write down a lot of activities that went on at the church in the beginning, but as time wore on and we became more involved, well, that meant that we devoted more time and finances to church activities mingled in with our projects and every day involvements. We quickly found ourselves involved with teaching and children's church ministries, as well as with youth activities – often using the youth to help entertain and train the smaller children.

On Sunday, July 23, 2000, we went to church for both services. The morning's service lasted until after one o'clock (the service began around eleven). The adults evidently had a glorious service. We had a "hallelujah" time in children's church, as well, trying to entertain 15 small children (ages 10 and under) for two hours with a

45-minute program...but we survived. We rested for a while this afternoon before going back to church. After the morning service, we definitely needed the rest!

On Monday, July 31, we got home from gardening and canning about three o'clock. We took baths and cooked supper for Brother and Sister Kelly who attended our church. She was a retired minister who had been very sick so we decided to take them a catfish supper with all the trimmings. They sure did enjoy the meal, and the company. After they ate, we cleaned their kitchen and went home to clean up our kitchen from all the cooking, before going to bed. It was a long, tiring day...yet very fulfilling.

Wednesday, August 2, We went to church tonight. Charley talked about the book of Ruth and it was a very good lesson. I could relate so well...*whether thou goest, I will go, and whether thou lodgest, I will lodge.* Is that what this cabin thing is about? Is this a Ruth/Naomi...Charley/Kathy thing? Well the ending is right anyway...*Thy God shall be my God*...we are in agreement here – so we can survive the rest!

On Monday, August 14, after attending Aunt Susie's funeral (see Chapter 8), I worked on children's church projects for Sunday. I also wrote a puppet skit titled, "Gunslingin' Joe," for one of the teenagers who helped me with children's church. He wanted to practice the skit before he did his "act" for the kids.

Gunslingin' Joe entertaining the children in children's church.

Sunday, November 5, we went to First Assembly of God church in Lawrenceburg this morning. They had a missionary speaker, Dan Webb, who remembered Charley's parents, and Connie. Charley's parents had supported Webb's parents (Robert and Dorothy Webb) for years while they were missionaries. It is indeed a small world.

Thursday, November 9, I went to an appreciation supper for Brother and Sister Kelly at Calvary Hill Church of God in Lawrenceburg.

Wednesday, November 15, we had to be at the church by 4:00 to help clean the fellowship hall and look at an order book to decide on what materials we needed to order to make items for the craft bazaar that the church is having in a few weeks. We got home about seven o'clock.

Thursday, I worked on the church craft bazaar by making 30 - 8 ounce jars of grape and apple jelly (15 of each). Charley mixed up hot cocoa mix (it took a while because I did not get exactly the right cocoa. I should have gotten Nestlé's Quick but I got an off-brand, so he kept manipulating the ingredients until he got it to the right taste). We filled up 30 baby jars with the dry mixture, and had enough mixture for about 30 more jars.

Then we cut out round pieces of material to use as covers on all the lids. We then tied red and green yarn around the covers. They looked very Christmassy. Charley also worked on some Christmas mugs. He put lace around the edges, using red or green netting inside and then filled them with hard candy. They are very pretty and I hope they will sell. We still have quite a bit to do. Hopefully, we will get it done before the craft show. The craft bazaar is scheduled for December 9, so we have a lot to do in a short time.

Saturday, November 18, we went to town to get more craft supplies. Then we went to the "Christmas in the Country" craft show in Lawrenceburg. It was fun and interesting, and it gave us some ideas for the upcoming craft bazaar for our church.

Charley went to the home of one of the church members to help cut up firewood for Bicycle Bob. It was very cold outside, but Charley said it wasn't too bad while he was working.

We went to church for revival, where we had a very good message. The women met after church to discuss the bazaar. I'm glad to see them working together. The high temperature today was in the upper 30s. Thermal underwear time is here!

On Monday, November 20, after we returned home from working at the cabin, I filled 15 jars with blackberry jelly and 16 baby jars of cocoa mix for the church craft bazaar.

On Tuesday night, the ladies from church met at the home one of the ladies and worked on items for the church craft bazaar. We got a lot accomplished, and had some good fellowship time, too.

On Sunday, November 26, Charley went to Lawrenceburg to speak at the Cumberland Presbyterian Church for the Gideons. He took me to our church on his way to Lawrenceburg because Shelly Ann (my puppet) was going to be at children's church. He came back for me after his church service at Lawrenceburg.

On Saturday, December 2, Charley and I helped make peanut brittle with several others from the church. We met at the home of one of the church members. It was a strenuous day but exhilarating. It was fast paced at times and then there were times that everything went slow. It was a hurry up and wait sort of day. We arrived at nine o'clock and were there until three o'clock. It took everyone working together to make 103 bags of peanut brittle. Whew!! Since this was a money-making project, sampling wasn't permitted, so Charley "bought" a bag for everyone to sample – just to be sure it was a quality product – and was it ever!

I, then, had to go to Lawrenceburg to get a few things needed for the next week's bazaar. We went to Papaw's where Connie had a cute Teddy Bear ornament that she thought would be good for our craft bazaar. She even brought us the items needed to make them – English walnuts, tiny eyeballs, and small fluffy cotton balls. It is so cute, and we feel that it will be a good seller for us.

We got a "skiff" of snow tonight. It was so beautiful watching the snow fall. It kind of puts you in the Christmas spirit with temperature in the upper 30s.

On Tuesday, December 5, we made peanut brittle again...106 bags! When we returned home I baked nine loaves of breads (cinnamon swirly, banana nut, and cranberry/orange), made up sourdough rolls, mixed up peanut butter balls (Charley rolled them out), and typed up this week's puppet skit for children's church. Charley made the rest of the teddy bears, worked on baskets, and helped me wrap and put ribbons and bows on the breads.

Wednesday found us fixing three different kinds of fudge, baking three loaves of sourdough bread, pricing our goods, and making signs for the church bazaar on Saturday. We went to Lawrenceburg to get the ingredients to make chili and a few other things that we needed for the bazaar.

At church tonight the ladies priced the things that were ordered to sell at the church bazaar while Charley and the pastor worked on the signs. Everything is beginning to take shape for the bazaar.

On Thursday, we made three more batches of fudge, four batches of chili, an Italian Cream Cake and seven dozen Friendship muffins. Charley was able to find us some mistletoe, and pine and cedar clippings. He also put up the bazaar signs at the church. We finished pricing everything today, and Charley made labels for all our sale items.

On Friday, we got everything set up for the church bazaar. There were only eight or nine of us able to set it up but we got it done. We are going to bed early tonight because we have to be at the church by seven o'clock in the morning.

Saturday, December 9, the church bazaar went very well. It appeared that the church made about $600 from the event. The turnout was not as large as expected, but I believe that is because it was not advertised very well. Everyone was too busy working!

Pat came to the church and bought a few things at the church bazaar. It was so sweet of her to drive so far to support our church. We got home before 6:30 yesterday and had to be at Calvary Hill Church of God by 7:00. This event was a leadership training for an area conference that was to be held at Calvary Hill. It was nearly nine o'clock when we left the church. It sure made for a lo-o-o-ng day...does the Lord pay overtime? (We already know that answer...*shaken down and running over* are our blessings!)

On Wednesday, I worked on my angel costume for the Christmas play. I spray starched it so it will be stiff and hold its shape. I am also going to put glitter on the tips since I am the head angel (with the most talking...and memory work).

On Friday we went to Wal-Mart and to Papaw's. We made two angel costumes for two of the little girls as their mother did not have time to make them. We did not want the girls to have different costumes from everyone else. So we were up until midnight working on those.

We have been up late every night for two weeks now, but we are fortunate that we can sleep a little longer in the mornings.

It's Tuesday, December 12, and I got my angel cos-tume finished today for the Christmas play. Charley made my halo and my wings...*I got my wings today, and I did not hear a bell ring!* I plan to starch and iron the wings again tomorrow.

On Sunday evening, December 17, we had our Christmas play at church. It went over pretty well, and I was glad that it was behind us. We had fellowship after-wards with finger foods and gifts. I am so glad it is all over. Now maybe we can relax and focus on <u>our</u> family Christmas.

Sunday, December 24, Christmas Eve. We went to church this morning. Bicycle Bob came home with us from church for lunch. I think he really enjoyed the meal. He put his mouth close to his plate and shoveled continuously for several minutes. It appeared that this was the first real meal that he had had in quite some time.

On December 31, 2000, New Year's Eve, we had a "Watch Night" service at church beginning at nine o'clock. When we walked out of the church right after midnight, we saw that it had been snowing and that the ground was blanketed with a fresh, white coat. The snow that continued to fall looked like glitter in the headlights. It was a beautiful scene (postcard perfect), and a reminder that the new year was starting fresh and clean.

It's Tuesday, January 16, 2001. I got the envelopes addressed for the invitations that Charley made last night for the Sweetheart Banquet at church. I also typed up the puppet skit for that event. The puppet skit is very sweet and cute...kinda like a "chick flick." I gave it the title "Romeo and Juliet" with only two characters, Katelyn and Scott. They talk about romance and different characters in the Bible and in movies. The boy acts as though he doesn't like the mushy stuff...until the end when he admits that he likes to see his parents kiss and hold hands. I think it will go over well. I chose two of the older teenagers in the group as the puppeteers.

On Friday, while we were at the cabin working, I found all the silver pieces that I needed for the banquet. Charley started the puppet stage tonight. He had drawn it out to scale and now will build it accordingly...as a good engineer would do! It is really going to look so good when he is finished.

It's Tuesday, February 6, and I have not written in my journal for several days...trying to recoup from the holidays. We have been so busy that it has been overwhelming. I have also been sick with a sore throat, and head and chest congestion.

Charley went to the church on Friday and did all the setting up. He did a fantastic job. I stayed home and fixed five batches of spaghetti sauce and baked brownies. Then I went to bed to rest.

On Saturday, February 10, we went to the church about noon and did more decorating, and Charley worked on the water. He probably spent an hour-and-a-half on it, before we had enough pressure. Several others showed up at 3:15 to help. If they had not shown up, we would never have gotten it all done.

I worked with the two puppeteers while the others continued to decorate and prepare the meal. Charley had set up the tables (on Friday) and put red and white tablecloths on them. Then when he had help on Saturday, they filled balloons with helium and put them along the walls of the "banquet hall."

The Sweetheart Banquet went over very well. There were about ten couples in attendance so we had a very good turnout...for our small church. Everyone seemed to have a wonderful time. With the payment of the meals, pictures, and donations we made $143 for the YWEA mission's project. We were pleased with that amount. We probably had more invested than that, but the unity of purpose of the kids feeling they had earned the money was worth the extra cost.

The puppeteers did a great job on the skit. I had typed the skit in large print, printed it off, then had it taped behind the puppet stage so they could glance at it as needed. We had worked on the skit several times, so they practically had it memorized. But we had flashlights for them to use, since it was dark in the fellowship hall (we used candlelight for the dinner), just in case they needed to look at their notes.

On Friday, February 16, Charley went to the fellowship hall at church and took the decorations down and put the tables and chairs back in storage from the banquet last Saturday. I really meant to help him, but I am still too sick to do much of anything. It really wasn't fair that he had to set up and tear down for the event (without help). Of course, he did not tell anyone that he would be working at the church, so no one knew to help him. He actually preferred it to be that way most of the time (due to his lack of hearing).

On Sunday, April 8, we had communion in children's church. Three of the children made the decision to commit their lives to the Lord. Now *that* makes working with the children all worthwhile.

On the night of Friday, May 4, we took a couple of the youth from our church to Pulaski for a youth rally. It was held at the football field and was a full stadium. Darrell Scott, whose daughter Rachel was killed during the

Columbine High School shooting in Colorado in 1999, was the guest speaker for the rally. Some of what Mr. Scott told us was so very sad, but yet uplifting in such a spiritual way. Charley bought me his book "Rachel's Tears," and I look forward to reading it.

Monday, May 7, found Charley and me mowing the church yard. It took us about two hours using the church's riding mower, Papaw's riding mower, his push mower, and our push mower. It made for quick cutting with both of us using the two riding mowers.

We worked at a church booth at the Heritage Festival in Lawrenceburg on Saturday, June 2. We left home at 8:00 a.m. and returned just before midnight. We enjoyed the day and the activities, but it was a very, very long day...and tomorrow is Sunday!

Monday, July 2, 2001, one of the elderly ladies in the church had been sick, and it was our turn to take a meal to her home. I put a roast in the crockpot this morning before we left (for Charley's doctor's appointment) so that when we returned home we would have the meat ready. Then we fixed corn, mustard greens, green beans with new potatoes, and corn bread. Charley helped me pack it all up, and I took it to the lady's house (she lived about 10 – 15 miles away from our cabin).

Thursday, July 19, Charley and I made preparations for the youth lock-in for Friday night. We worked all day and everything appeared to be in good shape. Friday night's lock-in was a huge success. Everyone had a great time. We took a hay ride, went wading in the creek at Papaw's, had a wiener roast, went walking, made home-made vanilla ice cream, had communion around the camp fire (at midnight), cooked pizzas, played board games, and just talked. It was after three before anyone went to sleep and we were awake by six o'clock. While Charley was asleep, a couple of the girls painted his toenails. He looked so cute with bright pink toenails. Then we fixed breakfast for everyone and Charley took all the kids on a hayride while I cleaned the kitchen. Actually I just needed a break from everyone.

We finally took the kids home about nine-thirty. No one wanted to go home because they had had such a great time. They liked the feel and spiritual aroma of our little haven in the woods...but we were ready for them to go home because we needed some sleep! When we got home, after delivering all the kids to their homes, we laid down a while to rest. Charley got a couple hours' sleep, but I was only able to get about twenty minutes because the phone rang several times. So I finally gave up trying to sleep and got up. After all, who needs sleep?

During the week of July 30 to August 3, we had VBS at church. On Friday, I played a clown. Charley did a fantastic job of fixing my clown make-up and it looked very professional. I had to lie down on the floor while Charley put my make-up on me. Sully thought I wanted to play with him and he kept trying to lick my face. Charley finally had to put him in his cage so that he

(Charley) could finish my make-up. Everyone thought that I did a great job with my clown act. I had to write the script and then learn the script so that I could perform the act for the children. I was "Kazy the Clown" and I was dressed like a hobo. It was a lot of fun entertaining the children, and the little tots really enjoyed the performance, as well as the adults.

Sunday, August 26, was homecoming at church. A group called "New Vision" did the singing, and they were very good. We did not have evening service as the afternoon singing lasting until nearly four o'clock...one of those "all day *dinner* and *singing* on the ground" days. Everyone was worn out by the time we got everything cleaned up and put away.

Doug and Shirley held a revival at our church Monday night through Wednesday night (August 27 – 29). We had an excellent turn-out every night and Doug did a fantastic job! Shirley also spoke one night. Her kin folks alone filled the church. I believe that she is the 20th and youngest child of her family, and most of them attend the various Churches of God in the area.

Papaw went to church with us on Monday night, as he had never heard Doug speak. And on Tuesday, Pat, Jerri Ann, Bobby, Geoff, and Kelley came for the service. On Wednesday night after service, Doug, Shirley, Charley and I went to Shoney's for supper. We really enjoyed the time that we got to spend with them during the week, and hated to see them leave.

Charley and I began going to First Assembly of God church in Columbia a few years after we moved to Sandy Hook (see Chapter 8). We continue to have friendships with several of the people from Center Grove, even though we have not attended at that church in many years. Charley and I believe that people are put in our lives for a season…and usually for a reason.

Our cabin as it appears today.

One of the joys of writing a book...is sharing the book. In this picture, I am talking with a middle school class about one of our previous books. The children were very interested and asked lots of great questions.

To me, the purpose of writing books is not to gain wealth, but to share knowledge.

CHAPTER 8
Other Activities

Wednesday, August 18, 1999, we took a day off! *(Mark it on your calendar – it may be our last).* We went to Lawrenceburg to do some shopping. Afterwards, we made apple dumplings and fried apple pies. This was our first attempt at making fried pies. They were pretty good for our first try. (*But we learned many top secrets to good fried pies, as we shared our "errors" with the southern pros around us.*)

We spoke with our realtor in Bowling Green to inquire as to any potential prospects on the sale of our house there. She relayed that there were none!

After another hot and humid day with temperatures in the upper 90s, we paused our day and went to church.

(Author's Note: We sit here today, January 16, 2014, in the comforts of a nice condominium tucked in the foothills of the Smokies, reading and working on the journals of our past adventures...in our younger years. We have become so engrossed that we forgot that it was lunch time – actually two hours beyond our normal time for lunch – and also forgot that it was our last day of work before heading back to the real world. We rushed around to get our pajamas off and our city clothes on, dreading the heat that we would be facing as we exit the condo on this bright sunshiny day.

As we stepped out the door, we finally realized that we have been caught up in the reality of our past experiences, and the deceitfulness of today's sunshine. We quickly retreated to retrieve our thermals, vests, overcoats, hats and gloves.)

Thursday, September 9, 1999 (9/9/99)! It was speculated that all computers could have problems today due to the fact that computers are programmed for 9/9/99 as a generic number for end dates. When we turned on our computer this morning and it appeared that there were no problems. When we watched the world news later in the day, it was reported that no one suffered any problems with the computers. It would have been a nightmare if computers everywhere no longer functioned due to the date.

Well, now it's December 31, 1999! If 9/9/99 did not get our computers, we are assured that Y2K will. Millions of new computer and software companies were in fear that all would vanish at the stroke of midnight 01/01/00. Why? Because computers used the two-digit format for month/day/year (12/31/99). The fear was that the computer would recognize 00 as 1900 instead of 2000, and a reset of the date would put us back in the stone ages...the days before computers...what am I saying – that was the days before automobiles! Many companies spent thousands of dollars for software that would correct the problem. At the stroke of midnight there were no errors detected and business went on as usual...but the software rumors sure made software companies billions of dollars richer.

On Tuesday, June 13, 2000, we made it to Laurel Hill Lake for a great afternoon of fishing. Charley, Papaw, and I caught thirteen catfish that weighed over 29 pounds. Papaw caught seven fish, Charley caught three and I caught three. I try hard not to catch too many fish so their egos will not be harmed. Well, not really. My idea of a good fishing trip is taking a book to read. I put my lines in the water and if I catch anything...well, that's a great fishing trip...if not, it's a great reading trip. Either way I win...and it's a great trip!

Wednesday, we are very discouraged at this time. We have not worked on our cabin for about three weeks. We have been busy with grandchildren, gardening, church camp meeting...and yes, fishing – Papaw always worked that into our weekly agenda. When we are able to work, it is too hot; and there is no air conditioning at the cabin because there is no electricity! Our years of working indoors have not prepared us for the extreme hot and cold temperatures, and we are soft from working desk jobs throughout the years.

On Tuesday, July 18, we got up at 5:30 a.m. again to go fishing with Papaw. Papaw caught five fish, Charley three and I did not catch any. Oh well, you can't catch them every time, but, I did get to read...well, when I wasn't relaying messages between Charley and Papaw.

Papaw always talked very softly (and often faced the back of the boat out onto the lake) and Charley could not hear. I would tell Charley what Papaw said, then turn around and tell Papaw what Charley said. I did this so much that Papaw finally said, "I can hear what he says. You don't have to repeat it to me." I got so caught up in relaying messages that I forgot who could hear and who could not. Did I say I got to read? Well, maybe a little! I honestly think that those two did not want me to read...they wanted all of my attention – for themselves!

(Note: Papaw would often ask what was said as if he could not hear well. But whenever we were in the kitchen and he was in his sitting room (three rooms away), he often could repeat everything we said (even when we whispered). So, Charley's hearing definitely was not hereditary as Papaw could hear very well.)

On Friday, July 21, Charley went to Waynesboro to get turkey livers for fishing and then he went to "our place". He said that our main spring seemed to not be flowing as well as it was. We hope that the water will begin to flow freely again. After all, this will be our source of water for years to come. Our garden spots along our driveway are not doing very well, as we are not there to water them every day.

We went fishing from four o'clock until eight o'clock. We caught three fish: Charley caught two, and I caught one. It was nice being on the lake away from all the projects and the garden. And, I was able to get in some reading for my relaxation. There were days that I would have liked to stay home to read or watch TV...now that's my idea of resting. Charley liked to go fishing, so a-fishin' we would go. He told me several times that I could stay home, but I did not like the idea of him out on the lake by himself. With some of these wild fishing tales you hear of the true southern fishermen, I worried that "the big one" might pull him in! And again, fishing got us away from everything else...including phones! Temperatures this week have been in the mid-90s and today it was in the upper 80s, so they are quite cool compared to the previous week.

Charley and I talked and he admitted that he was feeling a little depressed, too. It is not normal for both of us to be feeling depressed at the same time, but we both feel as though we are not accomplishing anything. Even though we are extremely busy with the canning; we are not getting any work done on the cabin.

(Author's note: Reading this chapter could lead one to believe that Charley and I lived in our boat...but keep in mind that this chapter is about "Other Activities" which included fishing as one of our escapes from the harsh labor of most other chapters. The journals would have been very confusing without topical breakdowns in chronological order to help our readers follow a topic from beginning to end...and thus the many fishing trips).

It's Friday, July 28. I took a Benadryl last night to help with all the tick bites that were driving me crazy with the itching. Unfortunately, I did not sleep off the effects, and I felt drugged all day. It was 8:00 p.m. before I felt completely human again and now it is 10:20 and time for bed, and I'm not even that sleepy. I'll be sleepy at 5:30 in the morning when it is time to get up, again. Ah, morning comes early!

On Saturday, July 29, Charley read in one of the local papers that one of the area electric utilities is looking for a general manager. We talked about him applying for the job and maybe getting our credit card debt paid off, but I don't think he will. If at all possible, it would be best if he did not go back to work. We do so much that he doesn't really have time to work...a real job that pays money, that is!

We hope to borrow money against the cabin after it is finished to pay off most of the credit card debt. Some of this is debt that Charley used to buy his retirement from Pulaski Electric System; and a small amount that we have used to purchase items before our house in Bowling Green was sold. It takes about one-fourth of our monthly income just to pay the minimum monthly payments. It sure is hard to have to admit that we are struggling financially. We know the Lord will provide.

It's Tuesday, August 1, and we slept late today. We got up about six-thirty. Wow! Today we went to Hohenwald to open an account for Shock Inner Prizes – a small business that we have owned since 1993. Through this business we sell a lineman print to electric utility linemen across the United States, Canada, and several other countries. When we got home Charley went to Papaw's to help him mow his yard and I canned five quarts of stewed tomatoes. Charley cut up the onions, celery and bell peppers for me last night, while I fixed our supper and cleaned the kitchen. Having those cut up really helped to speed up the process today.

Wednesday, we slept until 8:30 a.m.! I cannot remember the last time I slept that late. I am sure that my body thought that it had died and gone to heaven with all the extra rest. We stayed home and I cleaned while Charley worked on several projects. He called the head hunter regarding the information about the general manager position at an area electric system, and the head hunter told him that he had as good a chance as anyone for the position.

On Friday, we spent a great day of fishing. When we returned home, Charley cleaned the fish and I heated up leftover pizza for supper. I vacuumed the floors, prepared dough to rise for sourdough bread, and made a coconut pie. Both of us are worn out. I always wonder why we stay all day fishing when we know that we are going to be exhausted at the end of the day. Oh well, at least we have some fun while we are fishing.

We hope to get back on the right-of-way on Monday to start again digging our holes for the utility poles. Please let us get in soon, Lord. Perhaps this prayer is out of line, especially as we have taken some days off to fish. But we need breaks along the way, and fishing is a good way to spend more time with Papaw.

On Monday, August 7, after working on the right-of-way all morning, I could not wait to take a long, cool bath. I felt as though I had creepy crawlies all over me. After our meal I canned four pints of tomato juice, washed two loads of laundry and worked on a puppet skit for this week's children's church. I was tired and ready for bed, and it wasn't even six o'clock.

Wednesday, August 9, Charley finished digging one of the holes on our power line and was mowing the yard, when I returned home from running errands. I put away groceries and other items that I had bought. After Charley finished mowing, he took a bath while I fixed lunch. And then he studied for his Wednesday night class that he was teaching at church.

On Thursday, we were going to pull a pole to where we had dug a hole, but the tractor would not start. We had to jump it off seven or eight times, it would start but would not keep running. We finally decided to take the battery for the tractor home to charge it up. It had run down from all the starting of the tractor (and the alternator was not recharging it properly).

We went to Papaw's where I washed his bedclothes and his dishes. We then came home. The temperature was 101.2° with a humidity bumping 90%, so it was too hot to do much outside. I went to the Mennonites and bought fifteen pounds of tomatoes; Charley chopped the peppers and onions, and we made fourteen pints of extra hot picante sauce. We also had a rough thunderstorm to blow through later that afternoon. The temperature dropped from 89° to 70° within a ten minute period. I was afraid the wind would blow us away. That trailer rocked from side to side as if it was a feather in the wind. The storm lasted for about an hour. The electricity flickered a few times but it did not go completely out.

On Friday, August 11, after working in the field most of the day (see Chapter 4), we found a note from Connie inviting us to come to Papaw's to eat supper with them. She was fixing steak and baked potatoes.

I cannot remember when a meal tasted so good. We were so tired that I was afraid that both of us would fall asleep, face first, into our plates. The temperature was in the low 90s with low humidity. The wind blew most of the day so it was not too bad for working. Thursday's storm brought some relief from the hot temperatures!

On Saturday we went fishing and while on the lake the wind blew something fierce all day. The temperature was in the low 90s, but it wasn't too uncomfortable since the wind was blowing so much. Connie caught five fish, Papaw caught one, Charley caught five and I caught two. We stayed all day. We got there about eight-thirty that morning and left at seven-thirty that night.

Charley cleaned all the fish, and then we took Connie a couple of bags for her to freeze and take with her on her trip to Florida. We ate supper with Papaw and Connie. We had bacon, fried potatoes, and cornbread...simple, but delicious! We never turned down a "Connie Meal". It was so good to eat something that I did not have to cook. We got home about ten-thirty.

During the night I had an upset and cramping stomach. I'm sure it was too much fun on the lake, and then I ate too much at supper…I think Jesus called it gluttony!

Before we returned home on Saturday night, we had gotten a message from Alcyon, Harvey's wife, that Aunt Susie Vandiver was not expected to live. She called back about 9:30 p.m. and left another message that Aunt Susie died about 7:00. The funeral was to be at 11 a.m. on Monday in Russellville, Alabama. Aunt Susie was really a second cousin to Charley. She was Papaw's first cousin, whom he saw after 70 years at a Gandy family reunion in May. He was so glad that he had that opportunity to visit and reminisce with her.

Everybody just called her Aunt Susie because to Charley's second cousins, she was their aunt. A few years ago we met Harvey and Alcyon through genealogy research of the Gandy family. We found Harvey's name in the Russellville, Alabama telephone book. Charley called Harvey (a common name in Papaw's family), and while they were talking they realized that they were second cousins! (We enjoyed many visits with Harvey and Alcyon. Alcyon died several years later from cancer.)

Sunday, August 13, I got up with my stomach still upset but we went to church and had children's church as usual. We tried to rest during the afternoon, but it was a very busy afternoon for the phone, since we had to find out the arrangements for Aunt Susie. We also had to find out if Papaw wanted to go with us – which he did. Charley was also sick. Both of us felt rotten. We had to be better by tomorrow for the funeral. Maybe a good night's rest will help...and it's 10:30 p.m. now!

On Monday, August 14, Charley, Papaw and I went to Russellville, Alabama for Aunt Susie's funeral and after the service we went to a small place for lunch where we had catfish. It was delicious. The restaurant was on US 43 just south of the road that turned left toward Old Bethel Cemetery. The restaurant had a pond in front of it with fish in the pond – very unique. We had eaten there before with Harvey and Alcyon where we met several additional second cousins

We went back by Kroger in Lawrenceburg where we ordered a birthday cake for Bud's birthday on Saturday. We are planning to cook catfish and all the trimmings for him.

On Wednesday, Charley drove the tractor back to the cabin and put the auger on so we could get an early start on Friday with digging power line holes. The temperature at 2:30 p.m. was 102°! It was unbelievable!

When we returned home, I cut up about a gallon of green tomatoes for pickling.

On Sunday morning I finished the pickled green to-matoes. We had a yield of twelve one-half pint jars. I then got ready for church. Sunday afternoon we fixed a vegetable tray to take to a shower that the ladies were giving at church.

We are very tired. I have no-see-um bites all over me and they itch like poison oak. If there is anything I hate more than a tick bite, it is a no-see-um bite. They cannot be removed like a tick...you just have to wear them out, if they don't wear you out, first!

Tuesday, August 22, when we returned home from helping Papaw, the air conditioner at the trailer was not working again. It was 92° inside...much too hot to stay inside, so we ate supper on the deck. Charley got the air conditioner working, and our prayer was that it was fixed for good. The temperature today was in the low 90s with a good breeze for most of the day.

On Thursday, well, the air conditioner went off again during the night, so we called our landlord. She will send someone to fix it for us. Charley told her that he had got-ten it to work for a while, but then it went out again. I sure hope she can get it fixed...it's too hot to be without air conditioning, especially in a trailer!

On Friday, we went to a Lewis County High School football game for Charley's 35th class reunion. When Bob Burklow, a friend of Charley's from high school and a member of his football team, found out that Charley did not have a yearbook, he offered to give him one of his since he had an extra one. Charley was thrilled because he had been trying to find a yearbook for several years, and now, thanks to Bob, he had one. (Charley spent several hours looking over the yearbook reminiscing the good ol' days.)

Charley worked on his tractor on Wednesday, August 30. It still isn't running too well. One of the men from church told Charley that it was the coil. Charley talked to Jerry and he agreed that that could be the problem. Jerry had one so we will get it over the weekend.

Charley started looking for his tractor books. I am quite sure that he took them to the cabin. We can never find anything here at the trailer. It is so frustrating to always look for things! I will be so glad when we can move to our cabin and get things organized.

After a long, frustrating and hot day, we went to church. Temperature today was 98° - 100° with a heat index of 115° - 120°. Too hot to do anything...inside or out!

On Tuesday, September 5, Charley got the tractor running. The problem was the plug wires; they were not making good connections. Jerry gave him what he needed to redo the wires and they worked great.

On Thursday, when we got home from trying to set up a gin pole that had fallen three times (See Chapter 4), Charley walked into a board across the top of the shed. He hit his head so hard that I could hear the crack from where I stood on the back deck. His head bled some but we were able to doctor it, and he did not need stitches. And I knew that I could not laugh…no matter what!

We did not have the best of days today, but at least my attitude seems better. I guess it was the release of tension from when I laughed so hard when the gin pole fell.

Charley mailed his resume to an area utility today. It is in the Lord's hands. We have done all we can.

On Friday, September 8, we went to the Lewis County High School football game. They played Hickman County and LCHS won 41 - 8. They played a very good game. It was good to get away from all the tension of pole setting for a while.

Note: I saw my second snake today; it was a black one. I had just sat down for a break when the snake slithered across the bottom of my chair toward the truck. Supposedly it was harmless, but I did not spend a lot of time checking it out. I quickly jumped from my chair and moved away. Papaw laughed when he saw me move. He said, "I didn't know that you could move so fast!" He continued to laugh for a while longer.

If laughter is considered "good medicine" then we all should be pretty healthy because we have had our bouts of laughter this week…just maybe not at the right times!

Wednesday: Pat called this afternoon very excited. She had received word that Charley's name was announced as one of six finalists out of thirty-seven applicants for the general manager position at the area utility system. We will just have to wait and see.

Friday: Charley had a sick headache by the time we finished working on the power line, so we came in early…about 3:30. He took a short nap and felt better so we went to the Hohenwald football game where they played Harpeth and lost 26 – 0. To say that Hohenwald did not play well is an understatement! They typically are very prompt and efficient with their game plan, but Harpeth was an exceptional team as well.

Wednesday, October 11, we went to church after working at Papaw's today. Charley taught the adult class and he had a very good lesson. I don't know how he had time to prepare for the class, especially with all that he had to do each day. High temperature today was about 75°. Very nice.

Friday, October 13th: Charley was extremely sick this morning with a sick headache. He finally had to lie down in the truck to see if the headache would pass. He stayed there about twenty minutes and then said that he felt better. He still looked a little pale but he said that he did not have time to be sick with so much to do.

After a long day and not getting a lot accomplished, we quit for the day about four o'clock. On the way home he decided that we would go to Emerald's in Waynesboro for supper. It took us nearly two hours to go to Waynesboro and back but we enjoyed the time out. I really did not want to have to rush around to get ready to go somewhere. I would have been happy at home, but he wanted to go, so we did. He had a good idea as the evening out was good for us. I guess we were celebrating surviving Friday the 13th! As usual, I am tired. I will be so glad when we can slow down some as I don't know how much longer either of us can keep up this pace.

We are going to try to set another pole on Monday. We pray that everything goes well. The temperatures today were in the low 80s. Very Nice!

Monday, October 16, was a very beautiful day with temperatures in the 70s. The leaves have begun to change colors. They were beautiful! I wish we had more time to enjoy them!

On Tuesday, we took the day off, so Charley could prepare for his interview on Wednesday. Charley worked on his notes for the interview so that he would be prepared for any questions that might come up. He listed his accomplishments in Pulaski and Bowling Green, and made a list of ideas of what he would like to do if chosen as the utility's new CEO/GM. He did a good job with his thoughts and ideas.

We had another great day temperature-wise as the temperature was in the upper 70s. The leaves are beautiful with all the colors. The trees have gone from green to full color in three days.

It's Wednesday, October 18, and Charley went for his interview at the area utility. He said that he felt pretty good about the interview. But, of course, he won't know their decision for a while. There were thirty-seven applicants that had been narrowed down to six applicants. Three applicants were qualified with several years of management and engineering experience. Two of the applicants had two years, or less, of experience at small utilities with no engineering experience. One applicant had an engineering degree, but all of his experience was in public relations, and he was very close friends with the retiring general manager. The new board chairman and the retiring general manager were also very good friends. I think you get the picture! Three were "over-qualified", two unqualified, which made the decision very simple...and expensive considering the head hunter's fee to make it all appear legitimate.

On Thursday, October 19, the acting GM of the area utility called and told Charley that he did not get the position and relayed the same above logic. We had trusted the Lord for what would be best for us. I am kind of glad because I did not want Charley to have to go back to work, but I don't know what we will do about our finances. It just seems to be overwhelming. I feel as though we will never get out from under all of this debt and yet, we have to keep going. We just have to wait and see...and trust that HE is in charge.

Monday, October 23, was an extremely busy day! Charley and I got the gin pole set up for the last pole. We then went to the cabin and got some plywood and tools to make sides for Papaw's little trailer.

Then we used Papaw's lawnmower and got the leaves out of his front yard. He had a grass catcher for his mower so we used that to pick up the leaves, and then emptied the leaves into the trailer. When the trailer was full we would take it to the far end of the field and empty it. It took us about three-and-a-half hours to get it all done. Papaw had worked on the leaves about three hours during the morning, and we decided that we needed to help him.

Tuesday, Charley had a rough day. He fell once and scraped up his right arm pretty bad. Then he pulled his back. He had to do so much cranking and tugging on the hoists that he strained his back.

Note: As I look back on these writings I am embarrassed that I let Charley talk me into staying behind as often as I did. I should have always been with him when he was working, in case of an accident...or would I have been the accident?

On Saturday, November 4, It rained last night and during the day, today. We really needed the rain. I think Charley and I are going to do some work in the cabin Monday, because it is supposed to rain even more. We can at least do inside work there.

Today, Sunday, we had an interesting morning. When we let Sully out to do his business, he disappeared. We looked everywhere for him. Charley found him an hour- and-a-half later. Sully had gone up the road and was at the trailer near the entrance to the TWRA on

Smith Road. When Charley found him, two other dogs were rolling him around on the ground. One of the dogs was much larger than Sully and could have really hurt him, but he was okay. The man who lived there came out with a gun and told Charley that he "didn't take crap off nobody." He was upset that Charley had gone on his property, but then he apologized after he recognized Charley from our walks. It always pays to be nice to your neighbors...especially gun-totin' neighbors.

Monday, November 6, Charley and I went to Lawrenceburg to get the materials to make the brake for the reel of wire that we will be using for our power line. We went to Papaw's and had chili for lunch. Afterward, Charley worked on his power line brake. Papaw and I watched television most of the afternoon...well, Papaw napped, and I watched television.

Tuesday, November 7, 2000. Election 2000: Albert Gore, Jr. (D) and George W. Bush (R). It is a close race. As of this time, the electoral votes are Gore at 260 and Bush at 246. A candidate must have 270 electoral votes to win.

(Since the law of relations says you do not discuss politics and religion with friends and family...and you are our friends – since you are reading our book - I will attempt to keep our thoughts to ourselves. But I will say that Hermon and Hester Gandy (Charley's parents), were close friends with the Gore family. Charley's dad was also a big supporter of Al's dad, Albert Gore, Sr.

when he was in politics, because he (Gore) always looked out for the working man – Papaw, being a life-long union worker, business agent, and activist for fair wages for experienced labor). But, to summarize the election, Florida's voters determined the election. With the election resting with Florida Governor Jeb Bush, his secretary (and Florida Election Chairman), the U. S. Supreme Court, and the ever-famous "hanging chad", Gore concluded that he could not win, so he conceded the election to Bush on December 13.

On Saturday, November 11, we watched the UT football game. UT had 35 points in the first quarter. They set a record for UT for the most points scored in a quarter. They won 63 – 20 against Arkansas. The Tennessee Titans lost on Sunday by two points. If they had gotten a field goal in the last eight seconds they would have won.

It's Thursday, and it has rained all day. The temperature is in the upper 40s with 1.1 inches of rain. We worked on craft items for the church (see Chapter 7). Charley had a headache this morning and he had to go back to bed (the stress of working so much, then not able to do anything due to the rain, caused him frustration).

On Monday, November 20, Charley had to go to Papaw's. We had tried to call him several times but he did not answer his phone, so Charley went down to check on him to make sure he was okay. Papaw's electricity had gone off and his phone was out of order. We were glad that everything was okay. There is never a dull moment around the Gandy households.

On Tuesday, I cleaned house at Papaw's and began making preparations for the holidays. I worked all day at his house. I made spaghetti and cornbread for lunch for Papaw, Charley and me. Papaw kept his thermostat set at 80°. It was extremely warm, especially when cooking and cleaning. I told Charley that it was so warm inside Papaw's house that I probably needed to wear sunscreen to prevent sunburn while I worked.

Monday, December 4, we took the tractor back to the cabin. It was very cold driving the tractor...I was happy to let Charley drive the tractor while I followed in the truck. Charley also had to clear out a couple of trees that had fallen along the driveway.

Thursday, Papaw went to Florence for a funeral and when he got home he went deer hunting. He got a small buck that he said was for us. We will have it processed and have venison this winter. The 80-pound deer yielded only about 20 pounds of meat – that we received anyway – but it sure made for some tender meat!

Friday, December 8, we attended the funeral of one of my cousins today. She was 54 years old. I have also had a terrible toothache today. Charley stopped at a drug store and got me some tooth ache medicine after the funeral. I really hope that it helps.

Monday, December 11, I got up with a toothache again today so Charley and I decided that I needed to see a dentist. I called several before I could get an appointment. It was determined that I needed a root canal and the dentist preferred that I go to a specialist. The dentist was able to get me worked in at the specialist's office where he performed a root canal. The procedure took over two-and-a-half hours and $850 (which we did not anticipate). Charley waited in the van the whole time. He had gotten concerned that it was over an hour after closing, and I was nowhere to be seen and the office was locked.

In fact, they had to stop the procedure several times because I got so sick at my stomach. The smell of the rubber shield they put around my tooth made me feel nauseous.

After returning home, I went to bed and rested. Charley stopped on the way home and got us some strawberry ice cream and that settled my stomach.

On Tuesday, it was very cold. The high was in the mid-30s with snow flurries off and on all day. Charley went to town for me, and got groceries since we were out of everything. Why is it when you get sick, you are out of everything and need to go to the store? My jaw was sore today.

Thursday, we made peanut butter balls, friendship muffins, and sourdough rolls to give to the kids as presents for our Christmas gathering on Saturday. We worked all day getting things ready for them.

On Saturday, December 16, we met with the kids for Christmas (Chapter 6). We also got four inches of rain with severe winds most of the day. Later in the day we saw a double rainbow. It was absolutely beautiful. I always like rainbows because I am always reminded that God is very close to us and honors His promises to us.

On Sunday, when we got up, we had two inches of snow. The low last night was fourteen degrees. Now that is getting cold. The snow was beautiful. Church was canceled this morning so we stayed in bed until ten o'clock. What a treat! Sully and Fluffy really enjoyed chasing each other in the snow. They were so cute to watch.

Monday, December 18, we got up to another two inches of snow! The temperature was about 10° this morning. We went to Lawrenceburg to get a wick for the kerosene heater and a few other things that we needed. We got our kerosene heater filled and took the heater and extra kerosene to Bicycle Bob's house. He said it had fallen down to 12° in his cabin. I cannot imagine living like that. He had cardboard-covered walls inside with small saplings and scrap lumber as his outside walls, and there are large cracks in the joists around the ceiling – scrap tin being his roof. No electricity! He heated with wood which would die out during the night, and his light was a kerosene lantern.

He kept all his clothes on top of his chest of drawers to keep mice from chewing them up. He lived in very

primitive conditions. You felt as though you were step-
ping back into history, when you walked into his cabin.
He had no running water or indoor plumbing. By late
evening the temperature was at 10°, and it was very, very
cold.

It's Wednesday, December 20, and the low this
morning was seven degrees. It was two degrees at
Papaw's. As I write in my journal it is thirty-one
degrees and beginning to snow. The forecast is calling
for one to three inches. I hope not. We have had enough
snow for a while.

I rolled about 200 peanut butter balls today. Tomorrow we will dip them in chocolate.

Today, Charley has worked on his Dad's book most
of the day. I baked all day: Italian cream cake, divinity
candy, and dipped peanut butter balls...all for Christmas
at Papaw's on Saturday. I also made chicken and dumplings for our lunch on Sunday. I have stood up most of
the day and I am tired.

Sunday, December 24. Today is Christmas Eve.
Charley and I opened our gifts and so now Christmas is
basically over. Sully, Lizzie, and Fluffy opened their
gifts, too. Brittany and Brandon are supposed to spend a
few days with us. They're out of school and need a
babysitter. It should not be too bad unless the weather
gets to where we cannot get outside.

The temperature today was about 40° with the low of
28°. The forecast is calling for snow and ice Tuesday

through Friday. This is our second Christmas since our retirement, and we still have not gotten our power line or our cabin finished. We have been very busy with other activities...helping Papaw with his garden, his book, and other projects, along with other family commitments. And, then, there is our church involvement!

We may not have gotten everything done for ourselves that we would have liked to have done, but we would not trade one moment of our time spent with Papaw. Especially the time spent helping him with his book for his children. The value of <u>his</u> book? Priceless!

On Wednesday we went to Hohenwald to record our deed in Lewis County.

Brittany and Brandon spent several days with us, and we took them home on Friday, December 29, 2000. We had a good time with them, but now it is time to get back to work.

The refrigerator at the trailer had been broken for several days, and Charley finally got it fixed today (Saturday). We had been keeping our cold stuff outside in an ice chest to prevent the food from spoiling. (Just like in the pioneer days, except that they did not have an ice chest.) I finally got all the food back in the refrigerator.

It's Monday, January 1, 2001, a new year has begun and we have high expectations of finally getting the power line and cabin finished. We took off from working on our projects during most of December to work on the church bazaar, children's church program, our family

Christmas get-togethers, and the Gandy family get-together. We are hoping that life will slow down for us now so that we can concentrate on what we need to get done...and hopefully get moved to our cabin!

Today it has continued to snow all day. We now have about two-and-a-half inches of snow on the ground. It is a moist snow so it sticks to everything and is beautiful. Just right for making snow cream, which Charley made for us. Yumm!! Geoff even called and asked for the recipe so he could make some.

Monday, January 8, Charley and Papaw worked on the truck today. It appears that the starter is messed up, but they think it is fixable. Papaw is going to bring a bolt tomorrow (we had lost one), and put the starter back on. We sure hope it works. We need our truck!

Tuesday, January 9, Papaw came over again today to help Charley with the starter on the truck. They took the starter to Lawrenceburg to get it fixed, and now we have our truck again.

Tuesday, January 16, Today has been **so** frustrating. Everything that we attempted to do...we couldn't find the tool that we needed to do the job. We looked for twenty minutes for a tool that we finally figured out was in the tractor.

We are so disorganized and it is because we are trying to keep up two places. We can never remember if something is at the trailer or at the cabin. As Sheriff Andy Taylor said in an episode of *"The Andy Griffith*

Show": "I spend eight hours looking for a tool for a twenty minute job." Boy, do I know that feeling!

Today is Wednesday, and my throat is extremely sore today. I did not get much sleep last night because every time I swallowed it felt like I was swallowing a sword.

Sully has also been sick. He threw up on my bed and in his cage. I crushed up a baby aspirin and put it in some of his food. He ate that and seems to be feeling better. Of course, I had to clean up after his messes. So much for resting!

Wednesday, February 7, was beautiful! The temperature was 70°! Nashville tied the record high for this date in 1904. I am a little tired after being sick for nearly a week. It helped to get outside but my throat is still a little sore. Tomorrow is supposed to be another beautiful day.

I was still sick on Friday. Charley decided that I needed to go to the doctor, who said that I had a viral infection and a very sore throat. I already knew that I had a very sore throat. That was no surprise, but I was surprised that I did not have strep. I feel terrible tonight...pounding head and sore throat. I hope this medicine kicks in soon...very soon.

The temperature today was in the upper 60s with high, gusty winds. We got about an inch of rain. The wind really rocked this trailer! Charley said the church fellowship hall was rocking pretty good, too. (He was working on a church project – Chapter 7).

On Saturday, February 10, Charley worked at the cabin. I stayed home. I am still having problems with my throat. It has been better all day but then after we ate supper it started bothering me again. I can barely swallow.

We had snow flurries this morning with a low of 28° and a high in the upper 30s – a big difference from yesterday's high 60s.

It's Monday, February 12, and I am still under the weather. Once again, my throat is extremely sore. I have not done anything today. I stayed in bed until about 1:30 when I got up and fixed lunch. Sully has been puny all day, too. He laid around with me all morning, and now is laying around all afternoon in his cage. I crushed up a baby aspirin for him, so maybe he will feel better soon.

Charley worked on drawing out the cabinets for the cabin this morning. He took Bicycle Bob some wood this afternoon and then worked on his drawings some more tonight. At least he has accomplished something.

It's Thursday, I am better but I am still coughing a lot. Sully is still sick so Charley took him to the vet today. He said that Sully has a virus and gave him some medicine. I hope he feels better soon. Poor thing looks pitiful, and we miss him jumping around and playing with his toys.

On Wednesday, February 14, Charley and I swapped Valentine's Day cards. For supper, we had grilled rib eye steaks, baked potatoes, salad, snow peas (just for me), and homemade sourdough rolls. It was very romantic and sweet. Charley worked at the cabin most of the day, and I stayed home and worked on our taxes. Sully is feeling better. He actually played for a few minutes this morning and he sat in my lap tonight. Very good signs.

It began raining about six o'clock tonight. We have already had 1.2 inches since last night.

On Thursday, we had 2.8 inches of rain. The we got another 3.5 inches on Friday! That is 8.4 inches for the past three days. Wow! And now it is snowing with a temperature of 34°. Unbelievable! The forecasters are not calling for much snow, just flurries.

Sunday, February 18, what a busy weekend. After church, Charley had to put the underpinning back up under the trailer because all the wind and rain caused it to fall. He, Sully, and I went walking for a while. It felt good to be outside.

Charley started working on our income taxes. Apparently the Kentucky Retirement System had not been taking out enough taxes for the past two years. Charley gets two (2) checks from KRS (one for his Bowling Green time and one for his Pulaski time – each 15 years of service). The taxes were taken out of each check as if that was the only check he received (low income equals extra low taxes). But both checks combined, out of the same KRS office, changed the IRS taxes drastically!

The first year we had mixed my 401K in with Charley's income and paid with an amount set aside from the

401K – never realizing KRS' failure to properly combine the incomes to derive Charley's proper taxes. Ouch!! The end result was a $3,000 tax due!   Good Ol' Uncle Sam needs his money, and we have six weeks to raise it!

It's Thursday, March 1, and I have not written in my journal for several days, because we have been so busy, and I have been too worn out at night to write.   The weekend was busy. Saturday we went to Florence, Alabama to Sam's Club and Lowe's. At Lowe's we got the kitchen sink, a chandelier for the dining room and various other things that we needed for the cabin.

On Sunday, we went to church for both morning and evening services. We went to the cabin between services to check on storm damage. Everything was okay. We had had severe winds and rain on Saturday night. The underpinning at the trailer was blown out again and Charley had to repair that.

On Monday, March 5, after working at the cabin all day; I bathed Sully, baked two loaves of sourdough bread, fixed supper, and washed two loads of laundry.

A few weeks ago I sent an email to author Danielle Steel regarding her book "Journey" that I had read. I mentioned several of the things that I liked about her book. I received an email from her today thanking me for writing to her. I am greatly impressed that someone of that fame and stature would take the time to send me a note. Someday I hope to have the time to write a book or two *(or three)*. As much as I love to read, I would enjoy writing a book even more.

Wednesday, I stayed at home and packed away winter clothes. I also did odd jobs that we have been putting off. We are trying to get things organized so that we will have less to do when it is time to move.

Charley is extremely tired tonight from the survey work he did on Papaw's property. (See Chapter 5.)

On Monday, March 12, we went to Hohenwald this morning to deposit some money, transfer the boat title to our name (Papaw had given us a small fishing boat), and purchased wire for the conduit going up the pole at the cabin.

We then went to the cabin and put all the boxes, that Pat and I had unloaded, in the attic. We really have a lot of boxes stacked up in that small space.

We had to be back in Hohenwald by five o'clock to meet with Kenneth Carroll. We were to go over the survey that was done last week. Papaw, Charley and I ate at Big John's BBQ after the appointment, and it was very good. It seems we are eating out more than usual, but after all the hard work that we are doing, it is easier to eat out, especially when we are in town. Of course, once we settle into the cabin, eating out will be a thing of the past – or at least a rarity!

It's Wednesday, and Charley and I are working many hours to get things done at the cabin and on the power line. Both of us are pushing ourselves beyond our limits to get "The Vision" accomplished, so we can move.

Monday, March 19, I packed up a few more things tonight. Every little bit helps. We plan to move April 2nd and 3rd…less than two weeks to go. *(We actually moved and spent our first night in the cabin on March 29, 2001).*

On Thursday, April 12, Charley worked on the taxes that are due Monday (we get an extra day due to the 15th being on Sunday). Nothing like putting them off to the last minute. We work better under pressure…especially when we owe the IRS!

Monday, April 16, well, Charley got our taxes finished and ready to mail. We took them to the Hohenwald Post Office and mailed them at 2:30 today. It has been a very stressful day...paying the IRS is always stressful!

The temperature was in the mid-70s today. I planted a few flower seeds in the spot that I had fixed up as a flower garden. It was so warm that I removed my shirt down to my sports bra. I actually got a little sun on my shoulders and back and it felt so good.

Saturday, April 21, Charley's shoulder is still bothering him. He can hardly rest at night because he cannot sleep on that shoulder. His right elbow and his left shoulder are also bothering him, so he can't sleep well in any position. *(I think the pounding of digging holes for the power line is catching up with him.)* Even though he is in a lot of pain he continues to work on projects.

Friday, May 4, Charley started putting up the gutters. I took the van to get the front end aligned and the oil changed. We finally got to talk to someone at the bank today regarding our loan application. We began calling on Monday, April 30 and today we finally have an appointment for Wednesday, May 9 at 9:30 am. I am afraid that I went off on the person to whom I was speaking. The frustration of trying to reach someone for so many days was too much. Such a lack of professionalism and week-old voice mails is hard on this former banker. If you are going to be out of the office, you change your voice mail to reflect that. I worked too many years in financial institutions to know that you don't leave customers hanging. *Oh wait, I forgot where we live...small town...everybody knows when they are out of the office...and why – except us!*

Monday, May 7, After we mowed the church yard, we went to the Mennonites and bought ten quarts of strawberries. They were beautiful. We gave Papaw and the Bancrofts some and then we put up 22 jars of strawberry jam.

Charley is a low-key coin collector *(oh yes, in his spare time),* and he put all of his coins in cardboard sleeves and then into plastic sheets that he bought at the flea market over the weekend. He worked on his coins after he helped me cap the strawberries. He enjoyed working on his coins and he needed that distraction from all the hard work that he had been doing.

Thursday, May 10, one of the cats had kittens about a week ago and today we saw them for the first time. There are four of them and they are so cute. They will make great mice catchers!

Monday, May 28, 2001, it's Memorial Day, and it has rained all day. The temperature today was in the mid-70s, but in the cabin it rose to 80°. We need to get our air conditioner installed...soon! But the 10-foot ceiling helps to keep it bearable.

On Tuesday, we had two orders for Shock prints (Lineman: The Highest Profession). We mailed 25 for one order and four for another order for a total of $890. We had to mail them today. It took almost two hours to get the prints ready for shipping. We had rain again this morning. It rained 3.2 inches yesterday, and we have gotten nearly 10 inches of rain these past two weeks.

It's Sunday, June 3, and it has rained most of the day. Papaw was concerned that his potatoes will rot in the ground because the garden is staying so wet. We slept most of the afternoon...the soothing sounds of the rain on the tin roof lulled us into a deep, restful sleep.

Saturday, June 16, what a week! Charley's neck bothered him all day on Wednesday, Thursday, and Friday. In fact, it bothered him so much on Wednesday that he stayed in most of the day working on the plans for the deck. He has been in a lot of pain, but I cannot get him to go to the doctor.

   Monday, June 25, Charley finally gave in and went to the doctor. The doctor told him that his neck problems could be arthritis. He also had been having continual pain in his right elbow and his left shoulder – but the neck pain had out-weighed the others, so that was his "complaint point." He gave Charley some samples of Vioxx to try for several weeks. Charley also had blood work done and an x-ray of his neck. He goes back next week for a follow-up visit. He will have a complete physical around the first of August. Charley took <u>one</u> of the Vioxx pills when we got to the van since we had water in a cooler. By the time we returned home Charley had no pain in his neck, shoulder, or elbow, all of which had been hurting for several months! And the pain did not return to any of the spots, and no additional Vioxx was needed! He could not believe how much better he felt. (Of course, he would have felt better a lot sooner had he listened to me and gone to the doctor...but what do blondes know!)

   We went for a walk and walked all the way to Gandy Road at the end of our driveway. Our driveway is 1.1 miles, so that was a round trip of 2.2 miles which shows how much better Charley felt. Sully loved the walk as well, since he loved to get outdoors and roam around. Yes, Sully loved the great outdoors, until he heard the coyotes howling. Then he definitely became an indoor dog! We had a very pleasant day even if we did have to go to the doctor's office. Charley felt so much better and

I am glad that he decided to take my advice and go to the doctor. He also ordered the materials for our deck. So our next project will be starting soon.

On Monday, July 2, 2001, we went to the doctor's office for Charley's follow-up appointment. While we were at the doctor's office, Papaw called me on my cell phone to let me know that he had picked enough green beans for canning. I told him we would be at his house as soon as we finished Charley's appointment.

Oh, Yay! The canning season has started! Now don't get me wrong. I love eating and sharing the foods that we preserve. I just don't always like the all-summer process. When the canning season starts it does not stop until fall. After delivering a meal to a church family (see Chapter 7) we went to Papaw's to start the process of canning the green beans. The beans had to be washed, the tips cut off (we planted Blue Lake beans because they do not have strings), broken up, blanched, put in jars, and then put in a pressure cooker. We had enough for seven quarts which is one full pressure cooker. (Papaw said he had enough for canning and he was right!)

When we returned home about 8:30, we ate some fruit for supper. Then I put away the dishes and began packing. We leave tomorrow for church camp meeting in Chattanooga. We will return home on Wednesday.

Wednesday, July 4, we enjoyed the camp meeting but we were glad to get home. We went by Pat and Jerry's house on the way home to pick up Sully. When we got home we fixed a green bean casserole and mashed potatoes with cheddar cheese to take to Charley's cousin's house for a 4th of July celebration. We had a very good time with his family.

Today (the 5th) Charley decided that I needed to go to the Mennonites to see if I could buy some corn to put in the freezer. *(Note: The Mennonites did not have phones and neither did they talk to you or take notes for orders on Sunday...thus the "go" process!)* I was told that it would be a couple of more weeks before the corn is ready. And I was so looking forward to more work. Not!

Tuesday, July 10, was an interesting day. Charley received a phone call from the general manager of the Mount Pleasant Power System in Mount Pleasant. He wanted to know if Charley would be interested in coming in for an interview for the general manager position. *(The current general manager was planning to retire at the end of December.)*

Charley and the general manager had been close utility associates for nearly 30 years. Charley's name was given to him by several salesmen that provide materials to the power system. Charley told him that he really was not interested in going back to work at this time, but that he would come in for an interview so that he (the general manager) could tell his board that he had interviewed someone for the position.

On Wednesday, we went to Mount Pleasant for the interview. Charley said that the interview was very interesting and the job sounded promising. (Charley tells everyone that although he was not interested in going back to work, the general manager was a good salesman and made the job sound too good to pass up.) We will see what happens. Again, we are leaving everything in the Lord's hands.

On Thursday, after we finished canning the green beans at Papaw's, Charley and I went looking for blackberries to make jelly. We picked almost two gallons with which we put up fourteen 8 oz. jars of jelly. It was 10:30 when we finished. We were exhausted, but it was exciting to see all that we had accomplished for the day.

Charley also called the general manager at the Mount Pleasant Power System and told him that he was interested in the job. *(After much prayer we realized that this may be the answer to our mounting debt situation.)* Charley realized that he would have to be approved by the board before he could be hired. We are not getting our hopes up just in case the job offer falls through – again...as with the other area utility!

On Tuesday, July 17, the general manager called Charley to tell him that the chairman of the board thought that Charley's resume looked good, and that the resume would be brought before the board on Wednesday (tomorrow).

On Wednesday, the general manager called and told Charley that the board was in agreement with the chairman about hiring him. The board wants to meet him

(Charley), so a meeting has been scheduled for next Wednesday morning at eight o'clock.

On Saturday, Connie gave us a peck of peaches plus several more that were extra ripe. So we canned 16 pints of peach pie filling. They looked beautiful in the jars.

This afternoon Charley and I went to Mount Pleasant to look around to see if we could locate any houses that are for sale. There are not many, but we saw a few that may have potential.

Charley and I saw the place where he was born *(we found out later that where he thought he was born was not the exact place).* We also found the house where I was born across from the former swimming pool on First Avenue. My grandparents lived next door to us at that time. It was exciting to see the houses after all these years. My dad and grandfather built the two block houses around 1950.

We went to the Phosphate Museum to look around. We met Jimmy Dugger, the director of the museum, and he remembered my daddy and Grandpa Mosley. He had also worked with Charley's Dad, and brother-in-law, Jack Curtis, at Stauffer on construction jobs. I hope to talk to him more at a later time. There was also a woman at the museum who said that she was related to Grandma Mosley. I want to talk to her at a later time as well. They even thought that I might want to volunteer at the museum, when we move to Mount Pleasant. That might be interesting and fun!

We have had a busy day, and I am still wide awake. So much to think about and to be thankful for. Thank you, Lord that the job in Mount Pleasant appears to be working out for us. What a coincidence that Charley and I were both born in the Mount Pleasant area, and now it appears that we are going back home to Mount Pleasant to live. Life has its full circles!

On Monday, July 23, a realtor from Mount Pleasant faxed over some houses that are for sale in Mount Pleasant. I really did not see anything that excited me. We will need to go look at the houses to see if we like any of them.

We bought 12 dozen ears of silver queen corn from the Mennonites on Tuesday. Papaw and I processed the corn and put 25 quarts in the freezer. We worked very hard today, and we are tired.

It's Wednesday, July 25. Charley got the job at the Mount Pleasant Power System!! Thank You, Lord!! We need to keep our lives simple and get all this debt paid off. He starts his job on September 1 – well, actually September 4 since the 1st is on Saturday and Monday is Labor Day. We have a lot to do to find a house and move. Amazingly, we have to move 18 miles to be within the system. It is a ruling that an employee must live within 7 miles of the power system's office.

On Thursday, we fixed supper for a family in the church and took it to them. After we returned home from delivering the meal, I went back to Papaw's and swept, mopped, and waxed his floors and cleaned his bathroom. The house was in a mess after all the gardening and canning that we had been doing. Charley worked on our deck and is making great progress. Charley and I looked at six or seven houses in Mount Pleasant. We found one house that was interesting, and we will be making an offer on that house on Monday.

On Saturday, July 28, Pat came over, and we canned all day. We put up 19 pints of picante sauce, 10 pints of pickled okra, 7 ½ quarts stewed tomatoes, and 5 pints tomato juice.

In preparation for the canning, I sliced and diced about twelve pods of hot Louisiana jalapeno peppers without gloves. What a mistake! *(Papaw's neighbor had given them to us from their recent trip to their home state of Louisiana. She had said they were extra hot, but I assumed that she was speaking of eating...not handling!)*

My hands burned so bad that I could not stand any kind of heat or pressure on them. I washed and washed them, but I could not get any relief. Whenever my hands got near steam or heat, they would literally hurt so bad it was unbearable. I finally had to tell Pat and Charley how to process the picante sauce while I soaked my hands in ice water. (Even when I wrote in my journal many hours later my hands were still hurting.) Of course, Pat accused me of burning my hands on purpose so that she would have to do all of the work. (She was just kidding me...I think!)

Later in the evening, lightning hit a tree on the hill along our driveway, and got our phone and satellite so now we are without those.

It's Tuesday, July 31, and our phone is still out of order after the line was hit by lightning on Saturday. It was a very freakish thing as lightning hit the middle tree of three large poplars alongside our driveway. It then ran along the roots to the phone line that was buried across the road. It blew a hole in the road where the root met the phone line. It also shot large chunks of the tree wood and bark up and down the road beside the tree – one hundred feet each direction. Our satellite receiver, which was connected to the phone line, was also destroyed. We felt cut off from the world – again...well, actually, we are. In order to use our cell phones, we have to go to the top of the hill.

Our realtor called today (she left us a message on our cell phone), and we made another offer on the house that we liked. Apparently the lady who owns the house did not like our earlier offer. We like the house but it has a very small kitchen. We are leaving everything up to the Lord! After a tremendously long day, I am ready for bed!

On Thursday, August 2, we went to Mount Pleasant after we went to Papaw's and picked green beans, tomatoes, and cantaloupes. We looked at the house once more time. We still like the house, but the lady appeared offended that we would want to see the house again – and we are too far apart on the price.

(Author's note: Charley and I later became the very good friends with the former home owner. We later moved our church membership to Columbia First Assembly of God, and during the first Sunday School class we sat at a table with several ladies – one of whom was this "lady house seller." We all became very close and shared many blessings and burdens together through the years).

We found a house in the Sandy Hook community that we liked. In fact, there is a story behind that. We had ridden through the community earlier in the day, but we did not see anything for sale. On our way back home Charley said, "Let's ride through Sandy Hook again." I told him that there was nothing there, and I did not see any reason to waste our time. I felt so discouraged because it appeared that we were not going to find a house anytime soon.

But not to be put off, Charley said, "Okay. Let's put out a fleece. If there is anyone sitting on a porch, we will stop and ask if they know of a house that is for sale." So I agreed. Well, lo and behold, there were people sitting on the porch of a house. Charley got out of the car and asked them if they knew of a house for sale. One of the women said, "There was a nice house on the market for a few months, but they took the sign down a couple of weeks ago. The girl's mother lives across the street. Just stop and ask her about the house."

We went to the mother's house and knocked on the door. We asked her if her daughter's house was still up for sale. She said that she thought it might be, but she would call her daughter at work and ask. After the phone call the mother took us across the street to look at the house. We loved it! It was just the right size for us. The mother "sort of" told us how much the couple wanted for their house. The house even had an above-ground swimming pool – an added bonus for the grandchildren.

We talked to the husband of the Sandy Hook house that night and confirmed what they wanted for the house – a little above "mama's quote!" We may be making an offer on this house.

After our return home, Charley worked on the deck. He is really making great progress. Of course, as we will be moving soon we need to get as much done as possible.

On Friday, August 3, our phone was finally fixed, and we spent a lot of the day making phone calls. We had to call our realtor to let her know that we had found a house. She was not very happy with us because she did not get a commission from this sale. We felt bad about the situation, but it was out of our hands. *(We did send her a gift card thanking her for her help).* The one house that we did make an offer on (through the realtor), the owner wanted what she paid for the house, plus her debt above the house amount. This was several thousand above what the house was worth, so we rejected the offer.

We had VBS at church this week, and tonight I played a clown. (See Chapter 7.)

Pat called us about ten thirty to tell us that Jerry had died. We could not believe what we heard. Charley and I had a real job trying to get all the clown make-up off my face enough to be with the family at this tragic time. I still had extra-wide lips even with all the quick scrubbing prior to our trip to Pulaski.

Tuesday, August 7, we signed the contract on the house in Sandy Hook last night. It is a cute house, and we are looking forward to living there. We have been accustomed to one room for these past months and a house trailer before that, so it will be nice to be able to "spread out" again.

I canned four quarts of stewed tomatoes, washed four loads of laundry, and filled out the paperwork for the loan for the house. We have a loan interview tomorrow. (On Thursday, when the mortgage officer looked at our application, she looked at Charley and said, "I can tell you are an engineer. This application is filled out perfectly, and the printing is very neat and concise." [Was she flirting with my husband?] I wanted to say, "Well, actually the application was filled out by this blonde...and former loan manager, not the engineer!" But I knew that she would not have heard a word I was saying. She was too busy looking at him! Now it was my turn to say...just show me the money!)

On Monday, August 13, our loan officer called and told us that our mortgage had been approved and was waiting on the appraisal of the house.

Papaw gave me some pears that he had gotten from a man at church yesterday, and I canned 23 jars of jelly.

On Wednesday, when I returned home from spending the night with Pat, I could not find Charley. So I got in the truck and went to the bottom looking for him. He was not there, so I decided to go to Papaw's. As I was driving out of the bottom, the road was so rough, that I hit a sharp rock and sliced a tire.

I had to walk to the cabin and wait for Charley to come home. He was a little upset to find out that I had blown a tire. (No calling AAA! We can't even get cell-phone service in that part of the woods!) We then went to the truck and he got the wheel off and put on the spare tire. Now we will have to get a tire to replace the one that was blown out. Temperature today was in the upper 80s with low humidity, but it sure felt warmer than the upper 80s when I had to walk up hill back to the cabin.

On Friday, I bought a bushel of apples. Charley and I put up seventeen pints of apples and nine half-pint jars of jelly. On Monday, August 20, I put up fifteen pints of apples and twenty-two half-pints of apple jelly.

On Friday, August 24, Charley and I went to the Mount Pleasant Power System (MPPS) for a fish fry for lunch. We met all of the employees and really enjoyed learning about each of them. Charley is looking forward to his future with them. After lunch we went to Columbia to sign the loan papers on the cabin. It should be closing in a few weeks. We then came home, packed clothes, and got Sully and his carrier to go to Pat's house to spend the night.

On Tuesday, Charley bush hogged the road and around the cabin. He also did weed eating and the push mowing. I cleaned the cabin and washed the windows so everything would look nice for Doug and Shirley's visit. They came and ate lunch with us and spent the afternoon, so we all went to church together *(but separate vehicles as they were staying at a motel in Lawrenceburg)*. Doug was holding a revival at our church.

(Author's Note: Several years later, after we moved to Sandy Hook, Doug spent a sabbatical at the cabin. He said that it was so dark at night that he could not see his hand in front of his face. He actually enjoyed the remote location and being away from everything...and the refreshing that came with it! One of our visions for the cabin was to build a lake and smaller cabins around the lake and use those cabins for minister and youth retreats. That vision was partially fulfilled by Doug taking his sabbatical at our little cabin in the woods.)

On Wednesday, Charley helped Papaw with cleaning out his gutters. They did not get finished because there was so much packed in them (it had been a long time since they had been cleaned out). I took Sully to the vet to get his shots and then to Wal-Mart to pick up a few things. I then went back to Papaw's where I cooked lunch, washed and put away clothes, and cleaned the kitchen.

Thursday, we were busy around the cabin, since it rained most of the day. Charley worked on the computer, and I have been going over our closing statements for the closing tomorrow on the house at Sandy Hook.

It has been a busy week, and it isn't over. Geoff and Kelley have agreed to take Sully to live with them. It is going to be hard to be without him, but we stay on the go so much, and with Charley's new job we will be taking more trips. It is hard to find someone to take care of him while we are gone, and we don't like to leave him at the kennel. He pouts for weeks when we do that!

We closed on the house on Friday, August 31 and everything went well. The sellers cannot move until after September 22 because they had already planned a luau before they agreed to sell. We had hoped to have a pool party for the grandkids at the new house, but it will be too late in the season. Now I need to start gathering things to prepare for the move.

On Tuesday, September 4, 2001, Charley left for his first day at work (with wages) at MPPS. I felt as though my child was going off to his first day of school. I even had tears in my eyes when he left. It is hard to believe that he has gone back to work after two-and-a-half years. We have been together almost continuously, so I am really going to miss him.

Charley called once and said that he was having a very busy day. He seemed excited, but worn out, when he got home at 4:30.

On Wednesday, Charley was exhausted when he got home. He did not sleep well Tuesday night, and he got up tired. He had one of his sick headaches because his office was so cold. He said the air "blew down his collar" all day.

Charley fixed his air vent at work on Friday so that it pointed away from him. He feels much better tonight. In fact, he actually enjoyed his day.

Monday, September 10, Charley had another busy day at work. He brought work home with him. I went through some of our things to start packing for our move to Sandy Hook. (It seems as though we just moved to the cabin, and now we are preparing to move again!)

It's Tuesday, September 11, 2001! Today was a day of horror and sadness for the United States of America! The World Trade Centers (The Twin Towers) in New York City were destroyed by two hijacked planes. The planes were flown straight into the buildings. A plane was also flown into the Pentagon in Washington, D.C. and a fourth plane was hijacked and crashed into a field in Pennsylvania.

What happens now? Will this cause us to go into a Third World War? How will the U.S. retaliate? Who did this? President Bush says that "we will find out, and they will be punished!"

I have not accomplished anything today. I could not tear myself away from the television. There is no way to determine how many people have been killed. There are no words to express what our nation has gone through.

It's Thursday, September 13, and the horror of what has happened continues. More devastation as more buildings have collapsed in New York. Thousands of people were killed on Tuesday. New York City looks as though it has been bombed. This will be a nightmare for months (and years) to come. The world is in turmoil over the terrorist strike of September 11, and we are afraid that war is inevitable.

I met Charley after work so we could go to Columbia to get him a printer for work. They have two primitive computers with fifteen year old software, but no printers or fax machine. We also found a fax machine for the cabin.

Saturday, September 22, we have been busy lining up furniture deliveries and getting the phone set up. That was a trial. First the phone company said that we could not have service until the 26th, then it was the 28th, and then October 2nd. Charley had to call and speak with a supervisor to get the service by 7:00 p.m. on Thursday, September 27. I sure hope it is earlier than that but at the latest by Friday.

Tuesday, September 25, I went to Wal-Mart to get some cleaning supplies and a few things that we need for the house at Sandy Hook. When I got home I began to do some serious packing, and I have gotten several boxes filled. I have a lot more to do, and I will try to work again tomorrow. I confirmed all of our deliveries for Friday, September 28. Today's high was in the mid-60s with the low in the upper 30s. I hope Charley gets our gas turned on tonight, so we do not get too cold in the cabin.

Two weeks ago today the terrorists flew airplanes into the World Trade Centers in New York, the Pentagon in Washington, D.C., and they flew a plane into a field in Pennsylvania. President Bush has declared war on Iraq and Osama Bin Laden and his followers, the Al Qaeda.

Saturday, September 29, we have moved to Sandy Hook. Pat came to the cabin and helped us load boxes, furniture, and other things needed for our new house. She brought us a beautiful pot of yellow mums, and a rocking chair that we had bought at an auction two years ago. She had been keeping the rocker for us.

Well, our move to Mount Pleasant changed our lives yet again, but as we have said "we see the small picture, but HE sees the big picture," and He arranges all things for our good...so, we do not look back.

What about the cabin? Well, we do get down there on occasion to check things out. Greg uses it quite frequently for his "hunting haven." We do not spend the night there too often.

On our last trip down for an over-night stay, we decided that we needed to check with Greg to be sure that he and his family were not planning to use the cabin for the weekend. He assured us that they did not plan to be there, but later decided it would be good "bonding time", if they joined us for the night. Remember, this is a one room cabin with a king bed and a half bed. Needless to say, we were "wall-to-wall" people as we "enjoyed" the night together. Charley and I took turns between a lounge chair and my half bed. But we will forever remember our "close" night together.

EPILOGUE

Charley continued working at MPPS for eight years, and at the age of 62 he retired again. We now stay so busy that we both wonder how Charley had time for working...again.

I worked with the local newspaper as a journalist for several years. I met a lot of wonderful people, and from those connections, I have written two books (with Charley's help, of course). The books are historical pieces. The first book is about a building in Mount Pleasant and the effects of that building on Mount Pleasant as a whole. The building was the pivotal point in Mount Pleasant during the phosphate years. Mount Pleasant was known as *The Phosphate Capital of the World*. The title of that book is *"Mount Pleasant's 100 South Main Street."*

The second book centers on a German Prisoner of War camp that was in Lawrenceburg, Tennessee during World War II, and the man who was responsible for the POW camp coming to Lawrenceburg. The title of that book is *"One Man's Vision...One County's Reward."*

Both books are available at Shock Inner Prizes.com and Amazon.com.

Charley and I have been involved in local and community activities. We helped build the Sandy Hook pavilion and community center that is enjoyed by many throughout the year.

While working with MPPS, Charley designed the substation in Cherry Glenn Industrial Park and assisted with the purchase and design of the substation on Mt. Joy Road, which was later named the "Charles E. Gandy Substation" by the MPPS Board. He continues to stay in touch with the current General Manager and close friend, Derek Church, as well as all the other employees.

Charley's second retirement has been good for him (and me). We help our sons with special projects as we can. We take trips throughout the year, especially with Connie, as the three of us make great traveling companions. And we continue to enjoy our "Connie Meals" when we travel, often choosing to eat in rather than go to restaurants.

We also stay involved with church work, where I worked with the youth leader and youth for about four years during a span of time while the church was without a youth pastor.

We try to attend as many functions and sporting events for our 13 grandchildren as we can, and are enjoying watching them grow up to be fine young people with dreams and aspirations of their own.

Well, Charley fulfilled his life-long dream of building his own power line. Oh, and Kathy's dream? My dream was to write a book about building our own power line. So we both have fulfilled our dreams...mine had heating, air conditioning, and with no ticks or no-see-ums. Thank the Lord!

Life goes on here in Sandy Hook and we thank the Good Lord daily for our experiences of the past; His divine wisdom in our life's plans; and His blessings on us and our family – that are so abundant and above anything we could ever deserve...<u>but,</u> it's peaceful and comforting to know that HE is in charge – whatever our next chapter of life might hold!

Definitions of Terms Used

Bottom: A flat field alongside a creek or branch that is typically rich in nutrients for seasonal crops, but is also subject to flooding throughout the year.

Cant Hook:　A lumberman's lever that has a pivoting hooked arm and a blunt, often toothed, metal cap at one end used to bite into the pole for leverage.

Cant A Pole:　To turn pole so top insulator is either in line with the tangent of a line, or to turn the pole where the insulators properly catch the angle of the pole.

Gin Pole: A gin pole is a simple lifting device consisting of a single pole supported by guy wires (or ropes) and operated via pulleys mounted at the top and bottom of the pole. The gin pole is commonly used to erect a variety of structures, from radio towers to log cabins. A gin pole can also be used to drag objects horizontally toward the base of the pole. The device is limited, of course, by the location of the pole and the desired movement of the object to be dragged.

　　The parts involved in a basic gin pole are simple: a pole of sufficient size for the task at hand, a quantity of rope and a set of pulleys. The pole is set into a hole and secured with anchorage stakes to prevent movement. Guy lines attached to the top of the pole are strung out and attached to anchoring points some distance away; four guy lines are typically used to provide adequate support, but additional guying may be needed for heavier loads.

Keying a Pole: A pole may be "keyed" with a rock or other non-perishable object just below the ground line to offset an unbalance in a pole due to a small angle, a service lead, or a street light arm.

No-see-um: Mite that gets into the bloodstream and surfaces at random. Each effort to scratch the mite out results in his dive back to the bloodstream only to reappear a short distance away. The only solution to rid self of these mites is to use Betadine, or similar chemical, to coat body from neck to feet and not bathe for several days. No-see-ums typically come from aged wood or stumps that are found in the woods that are very handy to sit on when exhausted. The consequences of that rest can be long and tormenting. No-see-um...from the words (as supposedly spoken by Native American Indians) *no see um*...you don't see them. (Merriam-Webster's 11th Collegiate Dictionary)

Screed Board: This is a guide to keep the **screed** at the correct height so that the concrete finishes off flat. It can be a 2x2 board, or a 1 1/2 to 2 inch metal pipe set on top of stakes, that can be removed from the concrete after the first section is placed.

Upper Place: A field on higher elevation that lends itself to wildlife, due to the far reaching view of any on-coming danger.

ABOUT THE AUTHOR

Kathleen Graham-Gandy, a native of Mount Pleasant, Tennessee, grew up in the northern part of Giles County. Although her family moved from Mount Pleasant when she was an infant, they continued to visit some of their relatives there quite often. Her husband, Charley, was also born in the Mount Pleasant area on Mt. Joy Road. His family moved to Lewis County when he was an infant.

Graham-Gandy has a natural tendency towards history, as she is always listening for new stories about her hometown and the surrounding area. She and Charley have been working for many years putting together the genealogy of their families. They hope to publish this collection for each family in the near future.

Graham-Gandy retired from banking in 1999. She went from banking to building a power line as this book reveals. She and Charley have so many documented memories of their time together while building their power line and cabin, that they decided to share these with readers.

She spent several years as a newspaper correspondent of a small local newspaper in Mount Pleasant. It was through this experience that led to friendships with locals that brought about her first book (*Mount Pleasant's 100 South Main Street*). These same friendships led to the publication of her second book (*One Man's Vision...One County's Reward*) as well.

Kathy and Charley have a blended family that includes four sons and thirteen grandchildren. Graham-Gandy is involved in church, civic, and community activities. She and Charley are active with the Gideons International where both have served at the state level in Kentucky and have spoken at different functions. Charles continues to speak for the Gideons at local churches throughout the Maury County area. Kathy's hobbies include writing, reading, and meeting new people.

For more information visit the author's website at www.kathleengandy.com and on Facebook under Kathleen Graham-Gandy.

The History of Shock Inner Prizes

Shock Inner Prizes, Inc., was established because a print was not readily available that neither exemplified nor honored the lineman profession in the way that Charley thought it should. The name chosen was intentionally spelled "inner prizes" to indicate the special inner talents to be sold by the company.

So, Charley enlisted the help of an amateur artist, Dwight Williams (a water-sewer engineer at the utility where Charley worked in Kentucky), our small company was able to develop a print that portrayed the dignity of the lineman's work.

Charley wrote a poem that so appropriately describes the heart of the lineman, and the pride he feels in his calling. There are currently more than 5,000 of these prints in circulation worldwide. They are sold as retiree gifts, apprentice gifts when a lineman tops out as a journeyman, and appreciation gifts for storm workers after major catastrophes.

Many of these prints have been donated to spouses of linemen who have paid the "ultimate price" in the line of duty. The print and poem were spotlighted on a news segment in Nashville several years ago at the funeral service of two linemen who had paid that price during the Ice Storm of 1994.

LINEMAN
The Highest Profession

LINEMAN - HIGHEST PROFESSION

His day is swift, his night is oft long;
His steps keep beat to the whippoorwill's song.

He marches onward in search of what's down;
Dedication driving from comforts of town.

His one ambition: *Service above self*;
No time for sleeping 'til no work is left.

No "thank-you's" are needed to continue the pace;
The sole driving force is seen on his face

When weathered and tattered, it's still plain to see,
He's happiest knowing he's helped you and me.

For truly his heartbeat is "walking the line",
His muscles of steel; his bloodstream divine;

For in the Good Book, we read and are told:
What we do for others is bright as pure gold.

For the Master has said in explaining "the tall":
"If you want to be great be *servant to all*".

So Lineman stand strong, keep the pace, don't pause;
Your reward is with you, stay true to the cause.

Pattern your life by His 'til that Great Confession
Following your call: **Lineman - Highest Profession.**

Poem written by Charles E. Gandy
(a poem is included with each print order)

Shock Therapy